GRACE WITHOUT MARGINS

DEANA BOGGESS

GRACE WITHOUT MARGINS.

Published by Chart House Press.
Copyright © 2014 by Deana Boggess.

First edition: October 2014
Published in the United States of America.

Grace Without Margins/by Deana Boggess

ISBN: 978-1-63125-014-9

Cover design by Fuselli Art & Design
Book design by Carly Drake
Used by Permission.

Scripture quotations marked "KJV" are taken from the Holy Bible, King James Version, Cambridge, 1769.
Scripture taken from the New American Standard Bible®, Copyright © 1960,1962,1963,1968,1971,1972,1973,1975,1977,1995 by The Lockman Foundation. Used by permission.
The Holy Bible, New International Version, NV Copyright @ 1973, 1978, 1984, 2011 by Biblica, Inc. Used by permission.

TABLE OF CONTENTS

INTRODUCTION

"Where there is no vision the people perish."
Proverbs 29:18 (KJV)

THIS HAS BEEN ONE OF MY FAVORITE VERSES for the last thirty-two years. Fortunately, I have been blessed with vision my whole life. When God knit me together in my mother's womb, He gave me the ability to imagine, dream—and when I became a believer—to have vision. Sometimes I can't sleep at night, and often for days in a row, because God keeps clarifying my vision.

My parents cultivated in me the ability to dream from the first day I was born. They both believed people could change and the world could be a better place, no matter how many blows they were dealt or how many setbacks they experienced. This, in turn, would change the world to be a better place.

I heard the words of Dr. Martin Luther King Jr.'s *I Have a Dream* speech over and over again as I grew up and the meaning behind those words resonated throughout my home during my formative years. My parents' legacy lives on in our family. My husband Bill and I serve in special needs ministry, my oldest brother and his wife serve the homeless, my middle brother and his wife serve the mentally ill and the incarcerated, and my youngest brother and his wife have encouraged the chronically ill.

As a wife, I have been blessed beyond my wildest dreams. Bill continually supports me in whatever I feel God is calling me to do, and I am grateful for his partnership and friendship.

As a parent, I have dreamt many dreams over the years. We were blessed with two beautiful daughters and I dreamed they would grow up happy children who knew how to teach themselves, they would have great imaginations, they would be strong women that would be able to stand on their own two feet, and most of all, they would know they were loved greatly—by us, their extended family, but most of all, loved by God. Those dreams came true, but there came a time when our girls started developing their own dreams, and some of those dreams challenged me to grow. They have broadened my world, and as a result, I love even more people. I am so grateful for the things my children have taught me.

My grandchildren, they are my joy and delight! My hope is that this book gives them an understanding of the rich heritage they have. Hebrews 13:7 (NASB) says,

"Remember those who led you
who spoke the word of God to you;
and considering the result of their conduct,
imitate their faith."
Hebrews 13:7 (NASB)

May my sweet Jack and Chloe continue to grow up surrounded by a rich faith.

I am incredibly grateful for my job. I teach at a Christian preschool where I am prayed for, loved, and encouraged in my faith and as a teacher. As a staff we support each other. I have also been incredibly blessed by the parents of my students, who truly support me. They gave me the money to pursue my dreams as a writer.

I have had many "spotters" and supporters along the way. I am grateful for David Siek, Heidi Kantor, Wendy Kohman, Steffani Wilkins, Mark and Theresa Stone, Georgia Stone and Jennifer Smith for reading through this book and offering me much needed advice and support. This book could not have happened without the expertise of a dear friend, cheerleader, and editor, Diane Krause. She offers everything I am lacking.

Most of all, I am incredibly grateful for my relationship with Jesus Christ. He truly is my rock and the love of my life. He always goes before me to prepare my path and He holds my hand as we go.

Chapter One

SETTING THE STAGE

IT WAS THE '60S IN THE TURBULENT CITY OF WASHINGTON, D.C., and there were people everywhere. So, for most people, it was difficult to see the exciting things that were happening. It was different for me, however, because I had a bird's eye view from the top of my daddy's shoulders. Some people were extremely joyful and some were very angry. We were walking in the *Poor People's March on Washington*. On that day I was a minority but had no idea what that meant. I am sure there were other Caucasians in attendance, but I grew up thinking it was only Jackie O. and my family. I begin my story with that experience because it is the earliest event in my life I can recall that lays the foundation for what God would later call my husband and I to do. I look back over our lives and examine what God has prepared us to do. What is the special mission we have been asked by God to do? God has certainly gone before us and given us experiences to help us accomplish our mission and has gone before us to help us with the challenges that lie ahead. This is where I begin my story.

I was born in the fascinating '60s, 1961 to be exact. There were many ideals and causes floating around during those years, and people were very passionate about what they thought the most important ideal or cause was, whether it was free love or anti-war demonstrations. I grew up in a family where equality was the prevailing cause.

When I was born my father was a Methodist pastor in central Texas and had a circuit of churches. He would travel to a different church each week to minister to more people. Dad was an incredible man of faith. He had tremendous Bible knowledge, loved God with all his heart, and wanted to serve people, especially those marginalized by society. Early in his ministry he had the privilege of hearing Dr. Martin Luther King, Jr. speak during one of the classes Dad was taking. Dad didn't need to tell me how he felt about Dr. King, his life showed me how he felt.

After hearing Dr. King speak, Dad became more aware of the plight of minorities and had tremendous respect for what Dr. King was trying to accomplish. As Dad's passion grew, so did his disrespect for the response of the Christian church at that time. Being a pastor in a conservative part of the country, he faced a great deal of opposition while serving minorities. Over time having African Americans in our home became such a big issue that Dad eventually left the pastorate. Although Dad was no longer a pastor, I never want to communicate that Dad ever left the ministry; his ministry just changed form. Dad had a new path for sharing the gospel of Christ.

We moved to Washington, D.C. when I was three years old, and my father started working for *Food for Peace*. While we were in Washington, D.C., I vaguely remember the incredible monuments and history I was surrounded by, but the experiences that stand out in my mind the most were the riots and looting that I saw firsthand while we lived there.

I remember one evening my mother and I were crossing town to visit my uncle. There were people in the streets yelling, screaming, and stealing things from stores. I looked over at Mom to see if I needed to be afraid and she said, "It is okay, honey. God will see us through." And then she smiled. Mom's faith was a comfort to me. Today I see my mom as an incredibly strong woman with her own mission from God, but when I look back to my childhood, I see her as the reassuring rock in the family. She believed in everything my dad did, read every book he ever read, and reinforced everything they were fighting for with grace and fortitude.

My father's career shifted to working for the Equal Employment Opportunity Commission. In his new role, he fought for the rights of those that had been discriminated against in the workplace. Dad became one of my heroes, always wearing a suit, fighting for those that were not being treated fairly by society. His career led to many moves during my childhood, taking us from Washington, D.C. to a variety of places in Texas and Colorado. During my early elementary years I remember often feeling like I had one foot in one world and one in another. At home, we had a variety of people in our home most of the time including African Americans, foreign exchange students, homosexuals, and the poor. However, when I was at school, there was incredible peer pressure to only associate with your own kind, which caused me a great deal of confusion.

One of those confusing moments was in the third grade. A little boy had a crush on me and other children teased me about it. They didn't tease me because he was a boy, but because he was black. He called me one day after school and I hung up on him because I wanted to be his friend, but didn't want to face the ridicule of my other friends. My dad found out about it and immediately insisted that I walk over to the little boy's house in person and apologize. Dad was never afraid of the cost or consequences of doing what was right.

Gradually, Dad's caseload included more injustices towards the disabled. He fought for reasonable accommodations for the disabled and was involved in the background work for what would later be *The Americans with Disabilities Act of 1990*.

As a young woman I would often walk to the bus stop to meet Dad and walk the rest of the way home with him. He frequently shared scenarios of people affected by a disability and would challenge me to think of what the reasonable accommodation would be. I was always amazed by Dad's creativity and how even simple accommodations would allow a person to support themselves. Dad never set out to *teach* me how I should respond to the disabled; he merely let me walk the road with him. He set the example for me.

During college, God continued to shape me. I started out with a major in elementary education and then started adding special education courses. Over time, God placed people in my life that would influence my perspective on the marginalized in society. For example, I went to work for a woman named Frances, a stroke victim I served and tutored in reading and writing. In six short months Frances made an impact on the rest of my life. She taught me there are no roadblocks to communication if you truly love someone. There are only obstacles to overcome.

In 1982 and my junior year of college, I transferred to Colorado State University where I changed my major to occupational therapy. At the end of the year I came to a crossroads. I was tenth on the waiting list to be accepted into the College of Occupational Therapy, and I had the wonderful opportunity to go to China for a year, but an unsuspected third option appeared in my path and I knew it was from God. For some time I felt God was leading me to spend some time at a sisterhood. Through a variety of people and experiences, God confirmed over and over again that I would spend the summer there. A protestant girl just doesn't end up at a convent unless it is God's idea. My visit there proved to be one of the most challenging experiences of my life, but also one of the most transforming.

I wrestled with God the whole time I was there. I saw every dark place in my heart and I learned how to surrender to God. I was humbled by my focus on appearances and the disparity of my own heart. I learned to pray for every meal and wait on God to provide it. I learned to trust God with my future and give up control. During my time there I was surrounded by the godliest women I have ever met (and I have met a lot of them!). This was another way that God was preparing the mission that was ahead for me. I had to learn humility, faith, and trust.

Just three short weeks after my return from the sisterhood, I was given the job of my dreams, working for Lyman Coleman of *Serendipity House*. Lyman founded *Serendipity* and was a great Bible study writer and small group ministry trainer. My work involved setting up seminars for Lyman all across the country, and through that work, he taught me about publishing, ministry, and training. I had deep respect for Lyman and his philosophy of ministry, which grew from his being mentored by one of my other heroes, Rev. Billy Graham. I am grateful for the lineage of integrity that had been handed down to me.

At the same time, God led me to the love of my life for the last 29 years, Bill Boggess. He was humble and compassionate, and worked with those affected by hearing loss. God was preparing his path as well.

Bill and I lived in separate states but grew together in our faith through Bible studies that we mailed back and forth. We "dated" this way until I moved to California to be near him. While there, we attended Grace Community Church, where Bill served in their deaf ministry, interpreting on Sunday mornings and during the week for a Bible study.

While at Grace Community Church, God gave me a love and passion for another group of people marginalized by society and oftentimes the church: teen mothers. I walked with them in their fear, their loneliness and their feelings of rejection. Most of their families walked away from them, but some churches and the educational system were desperately trying to reach out to them.

Bill and I married in 1985 and welcomed our first daughter, Bethany, into our family in 1987. She was beautiful, had ten fingers and ten toes, and was every parent's dream. She was seemingly born healthy, but after a month, everything changed. She continually dropped weight. We saw doctor after doctor and ran test after test, but by six months old, she was only at her birth weight. The doctors told me I was an overreacting first-time mom. Exhausted and out of ideas, I called in the big guns—my momma. She gave me the strength to demand some answers, and we finally ended up with a doctor that knew exactly what to do. Bethany was diagnosed with *failure to thrive* and *renal tubular acidosis*.

We were given bicarbonate and told to give her the medicine every two hours around the clock for the next three months. The doctor assured us that as soon as the bicarbonate took hold, Bethany would change three sizes in a matter of weeks. We were scared to death, but the doctor assured us that she would be fine. God carried us through another experience of trusting Him and keeping our eyes focused on Him. Bethany has been healthy ever since.

Three years later our sweet baby Sarah was welcomed into the family. She was born beautiful and healthy and every parent's dream.

We took her home, but returned to the hospital two days later due to extremely high bilirubin counts. After a week's stay, she was healthy. Once again, we had to trust God and keep our eyes focused on Him.

In 1990, Bill lost his job because he refused to act on unethical practices, leaving us to stop and explore our options. We ended up moving to Houston for three years, and then God led us to Austin, Texas where He would show us what we were called to do.

Chapter Two

THE CALLING

IT WAS JULY OF 1995 WHEN WE MOVED TO AUSTIN and found our new church home. We were comfortable right away and soon felt the need to get involved in ministry. I tried a variety of ministries, including junior high ministry for a short time. After three months of Sunday afternoon headaches, I knew that I was **not** called to junior high ministry, but still did not understand what God was calling me to.

After reading some powerful books, I began to understand more about how ministry worked. Sometimes we are called to serve in a ministry simply because there is a need, and if God calls us to, we should be obedient and meet it. One particular chapter in a book really struck a chord with me. I needed to look back over my life and understand the lessons God had taken me through and as a result, understand what God had prepared me for.

Over the next few weeks I took inventory and realized that there was a common thread in our lives. Bill had been studying electrical engineering at Colorado State University and was asked to teach computer technology at a deaf camp for the summer. Bill didn't know any sign language, but agreed to do it. During that camp, he became fluent in American Sign Language. After that experience he changed his major to communication disorders and later became an audiologist.

I started to look back over my life. My grandmother had suffered from cancer of the larynx and had her vocal cords removed. She was able to talk by pushing air through her larynx and the vibration allowed her to make sounds. I had also grown up with a younger brother who was affected by cerebral palsy and dyslexia. When I went to Whitworth College, now Whitworth University, my major was education, and after the first semester, I added special education to my course work and made extra money by serving as an aide to a stroke victim. I also volunteered to serve as a buddy at camps for children living with a disability. After a year and a half, I changed my major to occupational therapy. Was it possible that through these experiences, God had laid the groundwork for what he wanted us to do next?

Advocacy was part of my DNA. I noticed injustice wherever I went. In fact, as a child, I often wished I couldn't see it because I always felt the responsibility to do something about it. I was also raised with sensitivity to the marginalized. I can't say that I always responded the way I should have, but it continually tore at my heart.

I didn't like the thought of anyone being marginalized by society, but as I grew older, I especially didn't like the idea of anyone feeling marginalized by the church. Since the 1960s the church has come a long way in welcoming people from a variety of racial and ethnic backgrounds, but those affected by special challenges are still openly turned away from the church—now, in the 21st century.

There are approximately 335,000 religious congregations in the United States alone. Out of that, approximately 300,000 are Protestant or Christian.[i] It is difficult to obtain statistics on special needs ministry. I have found the percentage of churches offering special needs ministry can range from 5% to 80%. Regardless of the percentage, we need to make greater efforts in welcoming this valuable population of people into the church body. For the family affected by special needs, parents are, at best, taking turns attending church while one parent stays home with the child. For the most part, however, they are all staying home from church because they feel they are not welcome. Many times over the years we have welcomed a family to the church only to hear that several churches before us had rejected them and told them not to return.

Over time I became more and more aware of what God was calling Bill and me to do, because of the groundwork that had been laid.

It seemed obvious to me. For Bill, the awareness of the need became more apparent and stronger. He had to respond to the need in some way. We felt led to this ministry, but we also felt incredibly inadequate.

Bill began serving in children's ministry by initially giving professional suggestions for children that were struggling. Gradually, he began serving as a buddy to a couple of children with special challenges.

Bill was using his gifts to assist some of the children, but it was apparent to us that God wanted to use him in a bigger way. It was at this time that Bill started the deaf ministry at our church home. He served in this capacity for a year and a half while I served in women's ministry. There were a handful of interpreters and a handful of hearing-impaired people in the congregation. He interpreted for Sunday morning worship and some small groups. The ministry was important, but was not thriving. Bill prayed over the ministry and felt that maybe he had misunderstood God's calling. He wrote a letter to the elders of the church and told them that he would be available to interpret when requested, but would no longer interpret on a regular basis.

At the same time, there were a handful of children that met for a class called *Joyful Noise* every Sunday. It was made up of about six children that had a variety of challenges. The teacher of the class was moving and approached Bill, asking him to pray about taking over the class. Bill made a commitment to pray for thirty days before making a decision. At the end of the thirty days, Bill felt God wanted him to serve in this way. As soon as he accepted this role, the deaf ministry started to grow again. Two months later, God told me to join Bill. I had no idea what I was doing and neither did Bill, but we did know that we were called.

---

i Hartford Institute estimates there are roughly 350,000 religious congregations in the U.S. This estimate relies on the RCMS 2010 religious congregations census. Of those, about 314,000 are Protestant and other Christian churches and 24,000 are Catholic and Orthodox churches.

Chapter Three

STRENGTH IN WEAKNESS

Bill and I stepped into our new roles, but we continued to question. We were excited about it, but we were also incredibly hesitant. It wasn't out of a lack of desire; we knew that we wanted to, but we had one haunting concern—we didn't have children with special needs.

We wrestled with that for months. Who were we to start special needs ministry when we hadn't experienced it ourselves? We had no idea how hard it was to have to fight for everything our child needed, and no idea how it felt to be rejected over and over again, even by the church.

We continued to question and pray, and then one summer day I ran into our pastor's wife, Cindy, and shared my concerns. She said, "You are the perfect ones to do it. You have vision and passion and desire. Most of the parents of children with special needs are exhausted and you and Bill have the time and the energy to commit to it."

Cindy highly encouraged us to move forward. Now, not only did we have God's promptings, we continually received support from people we trusted. Here we were, two weak and ill-equipped people thinking about serving in a ministry that we knew very little about, but we also knew that there was nothing else we should do.

Another verse repeatedly came to mind:

"That is why, for Christ's sake, I delight in weaknesses, in insults, in hardships, in persecutions, in difficulties. For when I am weak, then I am strong."
2 Corinthians 12:10 (NIV)

We were going to have to completely rely on the Lord, every step of the way. It would only be in our humble weakness that God's power would be revealed.

We started serving on Sunday mornings with a handful of children, limited resources, and a few extremely committed volunteers. Even though it was challenging, I wouldn't start it any other way. Every one of us grew tremendously that first year.

I think Bill and I had to be broken in a number of ways. We had to recognize our own limitations and how much we limited God. For me, any time I start a new endeavor I have to start off believing I can do it or I never get started. I can't even move if I don't think I can accomplish the task, so I give myself pep talks, prepare myself in any way I can, and get ready to roll.

The next phase for me is to realize that I can't do it at all. I don't have enough education, I don't have enough experience, and I seemingly don't have enough backing. As I humbly lie on the floor, stripped of any pretense that I can do anything, it is then that I turn to God. I tell God, "I can't do it, but I believe you are asking me to, so hold my hand and show me the way." My confidence is solely in God Himself.

"Now to him who is able to do immeasurably more than all we ask or imagine, according to his power that is at work within us."
Ephesians 3:20 (NIV)

As I teach my students each year, *it is only in our weakness that God's power can be shown, and then He will accomplish more than we ever thought possible.*

In terms of my partnership with Bill, I had to be broken yet again. I needed him as much as he needed me. After quite a few conflicts, we had to sit down and talk about what we are gifted in and what we are not. Only then could we be successful together. I needed to have his back and he needed to have mine; then we could be the team that God wanted us to be.

Finally, once we realized and acknowledged our own limitations, we had to realize and acknowledge how much we limited God. From this point on, any insecurity and fear would be due to a lack of faith. God called us. God humbled us. God would equip us.

From this point on, we would never be the same, because of the way people changed our lives and perspectives. We held on lightly because we didn't know the course of the journey God would take us on. We held on tightly because any journey with God is going to be exciting! I am anxious to share the rest of the journey with you. The stage has been set, the calling has been answered, and we have been humbled. Now the journey of growth, joy, and blessings begin. Even in the midst of challenges, we have been blessed.

Chapter Four

SETTING THE PARADIGM

I HAD BEEN WORKING ON WRITING THIS BOOK FOR A COUPLE of years and had written probably a third of its content before I even attempted this chapter. For some reason, this one makes me the most emotional, the most tense, and the most afraid of what I will say. I experience a similar anxiety when I conduct a seminar. Why do I even need to tell people WHY we should do this? It should be as automatic as breathing.

God has blessed me in so many ways, He truly has. But to be honest, I am a very simple person. I am no great theologian and never will be. I am often intimidated by intellectual people. As I tell my husband, my mind is one big room and there are no compartments.

The image I get in my mind is simple, yet powerful. Close your eyes and imagine this scene:

"People were also bringing babies to Jesus to have him touch them. When the disciples saw this, they rebuked them. But Jesus called the children to him and said, 'Let the little children come to me, and do not hinder them, for the kingdom of God belongs to such as these. I tell you the truth, anyone who will not receive the kingdom of God like a little child will never enter it.'"
Luke 18:15-17 (NIV)

Jesus is on a hillside, surrounded by people, and desires for the little children to come to Him. You have probably seen paintings of

Jesus holding small children and embracing them, but tell me: can you even imagine Jesus telling a child with a disability they couldn't be there without a buddy or that the church didn't have a way to take care of them? That they should go somewhere else? Most Christians are probably horrified to even read that and can't imagine it could happen, but sadly, it happens all the time.

Churches are not called to special needs ministry. They are called to embrace the people that walk through their doors, as well as the ones just outside their doors. In the fourteenth chapter of Luke, Jesus said:

> *"But when you give a banquet, invite the poor, the crippled, the lame, the blind, and you will be blessed."*
> *Luke 14:13, 14 (NIV)*

Later in the same chapter, Jesus said:
> *"Go out quickly into the streets and alleys of the town and bring in the poor, the crippled, the blind and the lame...Go out to the roads and country lanes and make them come in, **so that my house will be full.**"*
> *Luke 14:21, 23 (NIV)*

Those images are all I need. Jesus wants His house to be full, with well bodies, or otherwise.

As the special needs ministry started to grow in terms of number of children, we quickly realized that we needed to take the next step. I recently read this quote from Dr. Martin Luther King, Jr.: *Take the first step of faith. You don't have to see the whole staircase, just take the first step.* Indeed, looking at the whole staircase was overwhelming. We couldn't see the whole staircase, but we knew it was huge.

Thankfully, I have a husband that can see one step at a time and he is the great thinker and theologian we needed. Bill spent time in prayer for the scriptural basis of the special needs ministry. We both knew that we needed God's word to guide our steps and give us a navigational tool for the ministry. Over time these Scriptures have become guideposts in our perspectives. We share them at our training and use them as a grid and basis for our decisions and conversations.

The first Scripture is found in Genesis. God gives us His perspective from the very first page of the Bible.

"So God created man in his own image, in the image of God he created him; male and female he created them."
Genesis 1:27 (NIV)

There are no exceptions listed. God did not exclude anyone based on skin color, heritage, abilities or disabilities. He created everyone in his own image. One of the reasons this Scripture is so powerful is because it tells us that God made no mistakes. We were created and designed, as He wanted.

The second verse is found in Exodus. This happens to be one of my favorite Scripture passages. Moses was arguing with God. He didn't feel that he was the one to lead the Hebrews out of Egypt because he saw himself as ill-equipped. God's reply to him was:

"Who gave man his mouth? Who makes him deaf or mute? Who gives him sight or makes him blind? Is it not I, the Lord? Now go; I will help you speak and will teach you what to say."
Exodus 4:11 (NIV)

Once again, God makes no mistakes. Whatever our challenge is, God is in control and God will use it to do miraculous things. I think of Joni Eareckson Tada, who had a diving accident at the age of seventeen that left her a quadriplegic. I am often overwhelmed by the road Joni has had to travel. I cannot imagine how hard it must be for her to not be able to dress herself, go wherever she wants to go, whenever she wants. I am sure she has endured pain and a huge sense of loss.

On the other hand, can you imagine how different she would be—and consequently, the world would be—if she had not had this accident and allowed God to be glorified through it? Joni is the founder and chief executive officer of *Joni and Friends* and is an international advocate for people with disabilities. She has been such an instrument of God's grace, mercy and peace in her circle of friends, her ministry, her state, her country, and around the world. Joni's life and influence will be remembered throughout history.

The third verse we base the ministry on is found in the New Testament, in the book of Matthew.

"The King will reply, I tell you the truth, whatever you did for one of the least of these brothers of mine, you did for me."
Matthew 25:40 (NIV)

Jesus was referring to the stranger, the hungry, the poor, the sick and the imprisoned; in other words, those marginalized by society. When you look at the church universal, you can see that people with special needs have been marginalized and are "the least of these." I am asked to serve the least of these. How can I truly love Jesus if I don't?

When I reflect on these verses, I think back to when our house was being built. We had a plot of land and there were strategic stakes in the ground with string running between them. The stakes and string were not expensive, but were extremely valuable. If those weren't the right stakes, or if decisions for the entire house were not based on them, the whole structure would have been different. For any good structure, there is a starting point and everything is done in reference to those strategic stakes.

God is the master planner. God is sovereign and in control. God is the first stake in the ground. Any paradigm should be a solid one.

Chapter Five

THE CALL OF THE CHURCH

I LOVE CHRIST'S CHURCH. I TRULY DO. I HAVE BEEN MET WITH love, acceptance, and support there. Unfortunately, that is not everyone's experience. Many have been hurt, rejected, and abandoned there. This continues to break my heart, because it is so far from what Christ intended His church to be.

A new church usually stems from the desire to meet a certain calling or need and starts to take form from there. Ministries start to emerge, such as men's and women's ministries, children's ministry, worship ministry, youth ministry, and others. They are all valuable and valid ministries. Over time, staff is hired, rooms are reserved, budgets are established, and the ministry starts to take form. Everything starts to fit into a nice and neat little grid and people know where they belong. Then lo and behold, one day, a child or an adult with a special need walks into the church. People take a second look and sometimes say hurtful things without even knowing it. There's no place to put this person; people don't know what to say. The person with special needs may start bumping into ministry areas all over the church and people are left bewildered at what to do. There's now a person that doesn't fit into the nice little grid that has been established. They may make things unpredictable and uncomfortable.

The sad mistake that church after church makes is deciding that a person with special needs does not fit into their church, and they excuse it by saying they are not equipped to help someone with special needs. If you are a church, with walls or no walls, staff or no staff, but consider yourself a church, *you **are** equipped to serve these people*! Granted, we have had to adapt our accommodations at times to protect the safety of all children, but we have always prayed and adapted to make it work. Christ's church is for everyone.

You can have a special needs ministry with the presence of only one person. In those early years we did not have a staff person, a budget, supplies, or even a room, but we did have a hallway. Even if all you have is a hallway and you are able to love a child, tell them about Jesus, and allow his/her parents to attend worship, you have an important ministry. So many families have not had the freedom to attend church for years because they have to take turns attending to a child with special needs. Or worse, they have been asked to leave a church.

Over the course of those first few years we moved from walking children in hallways to a corner of an office, separated by a partition. We went to different classrooms and asked for toys that weren't being used to add to our classroom. We weren't an organized ministry yet, but we were a spot on the grid!

Eventually a room opened up in children's ministry, so we moved into our own space at the end of the hall, and people started bringing supplies to us. We placed a gate across the door to our classroom, which kept our children safe, but allowed them to wave to people out in the hallway. Soon, one teacher stopped and paid attention to the children, and then others started to catch on. We had many hurdles to overcome, but we were now on the map!

A few years later, a new worship center and education building were built and the children's ministry pastor wanted us to have a room up front so that people would be aware of the ministry. Money was allocated to purchase supplies. I was now on staff as a preschool director and volunteer director for special needs. We felt overwhelmed at times by our lack of experience, but at the same time, we felt incredibly blessed.

Chapter Six

PARTNERING WITH LEADERS

WE HAVE HAD OUR TRIALS IN MINISTRY, BUT GETTING THE leaders of the church on board was never an issue. In the early years, the children's ministry pastor wanted us to just tell him what we needed and he would get it. He checked on us every Sunday morning and was extremely supportive. He trusted us with the ministry and gave us a great deal of freedom. When it came time for the new worship center and education center to be built, he told us he wanted the special needs room right up front so people were sure to know that we were there for the special needs community.

Our senior pastor was supportive from the very start and this set the tone for the rest of the church. All we had to do was ask and he would get us what we needed. I remember many years ago one of "our kids" pulled the fire alarm on a Sunday morning. This was not a small incident since 5,000 people had to be evacuated. I will never forget the next day when I ran into the senior pastor in the copy room. We both looked at each other, smiled, laughed and then he shrugged his shoulders and said, "It happens."

We took the blessing of staff support for granted until we started attending seminars across the country. By far, the majority of the churches we encountered struggled with getting support from their pastor.

Sadly, prayer is often the first thing to go in getting a ministry off the ground. We may start there, but tend to leave it out when we need it the most. We had to continually remind ourselves it is not our ministry; it is God's. We needed to continually pray for His will and His direction. He is sovereign over what should happen in the ministry. He had already prepared a plan.

As much as you may feel drawn and passionate about this ministry, it is still only one of the ministries of the church. Each ministry is important and hopefully has the goal of reaching people for Christ. Think bigger than your ministry and remember that all ministries need budget, space, and volunteers. Each of them may be vying for the attention of the senior pastor or governing board. It is important to work together for God's provision and timing.

I recall a training we held where a participant came in upset and almost in tears because their special needs ministry had been denied a room by church leaders. Just because your request gets turned down does not mean that the leadership is not supportive. Sometimes a church has to grow into a ministry.

Be passionate but gracious. I cannot express this enough. God gave you a passion. Yea, God!! You should be passionate about special needs ministry everywhere you go. Introduce children affected by disability to the leaders of the church, to the new Sunday school teacher, and to the person in the hallway. Show the leadership your excitement and love for them, but also know when it is time to be gracious. Step back and periodically thank the church for the support they have given. Even if it is for just one donated toy, thank them. God will not leave you hanging. He is going to provide.

If you are a parent with a child that is affected by a disability and you are heading up this ministry, please be patient. Understandably, you have had to fight everywhere you go for your child. Whether you have been at the doctor's office, the school, or the grocery store, you have probably had to fight for or protect your child in one way or another. Don't go into the church ready for a fight. Be patient. Be passionate. Be gracious. God is in control.

~ 23 ~

If you are leading the ministry or are a leader of the church and do not have a child affected by a disability, remember that you haven't walked their walk. You don't really know the trials they have faced or the rejection they have felt. Be patient. Be passionate. Be gracious. God is in control.

Chapter Seven

SERVING VOLUNTEERS

IN 1997, WHEN BILL AND I FIRST BECAME INVOLVED IN THE ministry, our special needs staff was an audiologist, a physical therapist, a Sunday school teacher and business man, and myself, a stay-at-home mom. We respectfully refer to it as the beginnings of a very bad joke. None of us truly knew what we were doing, but we knew that we were called there and we were committed to the kids.

Of course, when you become involved in a ministry you want to do the very best you can. We had grand ideas of how we would structure the class. We would not only be able to communicate with every child, but would also convert them, heal the wounds of their family, and the whole church would instantly be on board. I guess I can't say that every volunteer felt that way. I have always been an idealist. Thankfully, my husband is a realist who helps keep things in balance.

I desperately wanted to feel close to every child, instantly. That is just how I am wired. It didn't take long, however, before I had to change my expectations. If the children left our special needs class safe, healthy, and loved on, if they had heard the name of Jesus and their parents had been able to attend worship, it was successful. As a starting place, this should be acceptable. All children need a little extra love from people outside the family. You can never hear the love and grace of the gospel too much, and parents should be able to attend a function together and not have to worry. The bonus would be to attend worship together. This is valuable!

It was always Bill's and my desire that we would build up volunteers that were trained and ready to go. They would be waiting to buddy with a child that had just walked through the doors. In fact, we were sure that we would have so many volunteers we wouldn't know what to do with them. It was a nice thought, but it just didn't happen that way.

We often had people ask us what the qualifications were to be a B.U.D.D.Y. (Building Up Disciples in Disabled Youth). We would laugh and say, "Are you breathing?" We always made sure that a volunteer could pass a background check, however, and in the beginning we only had adults working with the children. We prayed and we trusted that God would provide whatever we needed and He did! We never had volunteers waiting in the wings, but we always had exactly what we needed. Many times we would have a visitor on a Sunday, and within moments we would have someone come and volunteer to serve. Seriously, God always provided what we needed.

Over time, people with hearts of mercy gravitated to the ministry. They didn't necessarily have professional skills, they were just merciful people. We were so busy in the beginning that we didn't really advertise that we needed volunteers. We just did what we needed to do and loved on the kids. We had people from all kinds of backgrounds and professions serving with us. God always seemed to bring people with the exact skill sets we needed at the time. It felt like miracle after miracle as God brought people to our classroom. You never know who your most effective volunteer is going to be. We learned not to put our own filters on when we were recruiting. God can use and call a variety of personalities and backgrounds.

We quickly became aware of a huge need to be met. We saw that the parents we were serving needed respite care. Thus, *Parents Night Out* was started. Once a month we offered to take care of the children for several hours. Our evening with them was very special. We had worship music, played games, played outside, and had a Bible lesson. It was relaxed and crazy and FUN!

One of the blessings we enjoyed was to have our daughters serve alongside us. In the beginning of the program, our girls were ages seven and ten. They had a lot of energy, excitement, and love to share with the kids. Over time they started inviting their friends to join us, and gradually we had twenty different youth helping us at *Parents Night Out*. This became a bonus ministry. After *Parents Night Out*, Bill and I would treat the youth to a hamburger or soda. We would talk and laugh and have fun, but most of the time they wanted to ask questions about different children in the ministry. They just wanted to understand them better and learn better ways to support them. Those kids are now in their twenties and many of them have shared with us in the impact the ministry had on them. I have so many fond memories of those days and I know it has made an impact on our own children.

As a result of that experience, we started to use more and more youth as buddies in the self-contained classroom, as well as typical classrooms. They have energy, excitement, and are invaluable to influencing the culture of the church.

Over the years we did experience a few blips. I think some of the obstacles we encountered are pretty typical. At one time we had an influx of special education teachers that wanted to serve in the ministry. What a valuable asset they are! However, the challenge comes in their desire to educate, and they often are in an educational mindset, when you are in a ministry mindset. In other words, you have completely different goals. They may all be great goals, but there is a limited amount of time on a Sunday morning. This may not seem like a big issue, but it can be. It will affect the focus of the ministry and the priorities of a Sunday morning. This is also true of physical therapists, occupational therapists, and other paraprofessional volunteers. Everyone brings great skills, motivations and desires to the ministry, but you have to be able to focus on one set of goals.

In addition, a variety of people are going to bring great ideas for the ministry to the table. Many are good and may have a powerful impact, but again, it's important to keep the ministry focused. To do this there must be a captain of the ship. The captain needs to remain at the helm; otherwise the ship will start to sink with too much cargo and risks getting lost if it frequently changes direction. Prayer and focus is the antidote. Trust God with direction until He leads you differently; keep your focus where He has led.

In 2002 I joined the children's ministry staff at Hill Country Bible Church as a preschool coach and was a volunteer staff representative for the special needs ministry. I enjoyed serving as a preschool coach and learned invaluable skills while I served in that capacity. It was very beneficial to have a representative for special needs ministry on the staff team; otherwise, it was easy for it to get lost in the midst of a variety of programs.

In 2003, I became the volunteer director as well as the special needs director. The job had grown tremendously, but it was great to be able to focus on recruiting volunteers for all of children's ministries. During that time we had the opportunity to promote children's ministry in the worship service in hopes of recruiting additional volunteers. We had professional five-minute videos made, presented testimonials from volunteers, and invited church members to brunches and presentations on children's ministry. We also participated in ministry fairs, made appearances and pleas at ministry seminars, and posted needs in the church bulletin. Through these activities, we were able to acquire a healthy number of volunteers every year. In addition, we were able to maintain a presence in the midst of a large number of ministries in the church.

No matter how incredible our recruiting efforts were, they needed to be ongoing. My experience is that recruiting is not an issue that can be solved or eradicated. You merely become more efficient at it.

The next step in the process is training and encouraging volunteers. It is tremendously important for volunteers to be continually mindful of the vision of the ministry. Volunteers need to know **why** they are doing what they are doing. They need insight into the life of the special needs family so they can empathize and know they are making a difference. They need to know that the captain of the ship is guiding them where they want to go.

There are a variety of ways to keep vision in front of volunteers. Our children's ministry met once a month for an activity we called *Vision High*. At each meeting the children's ministry pastor would share with the volunteers where he was heading in the ministry. He poured into their lives spiritually and encouraged the team. After he finished and everyone had a time of fellowship, the volunteers broke out into specific ministry area groups to hear the vision for that particular part of the ministry. This was our time to meet with our volunteers for the special needs ministry to cast vision, encourage, and train. We also had a monthly meeting for the leadership team of each area in children's ministry. Vision, encouragement, and training were shared there as well.

Encouragement can come in a variety of ways. Regular emails help with vision and encouragement, although I advise keeping them brief. Lengthy emails often go unread.

Over the years we have given a variety of gifts to our volunteers. They were never expensive, but provided a little encouragement. Some of them were tied to vision and some were tied to spiritual growth.

Here are some examples of gifts of vision:

A journal for buddies to write down stories about the child they are serving.

A picture of an elephant sheltering a baby elephant, with a note.

A stone heart with cracks and blemishes to illustrate that we all have cracks and blemishes.

Some examples of gifts of spiritual encouragement:

A devotional book.

Books of spiritual reference.

A cross that could be hung on a wall.

One of the more useful tools for encouraging volunteers is a great time of celebration! Be sure to frequently share what God is doing in the life of the ministry. Share the stories. Share the ways lives have been changed in the children, their families, and in volunteers.

We have had two large celebrations in the last fifteen years. When the special needs ministry was celebrating its 15th anniversary, we called together all of the volunteers and all of the families that we had ever served. Remarkably, after looking through the records, we discovered that there were 100 volunteers and 100 children and their families who had participated in the ministry during those 15 years. What an extra blessing to have the numbers turn out that way!

We came together to celebrate what God had done. So often we don't even realize how much God has done until we take the time to stop, reflect and celebrate. When we had our celebration we decorated the room with large black and white photographs of the children. The event program was designed in black and white with a touch of red, and so was the cake.

We took the time to honor the volunteers that had made such an impact. The first person honored was the very first volunteer who had served for over twenty years with the same child. The volunteer, Laura Davenport, was honored because it was on her heart that God first laid the vision and passion for the special needs ministry. There were so many people to honor for a variety of reasons. We had a time of vision casting and celebration. At the end of the program we brought in all of the children that had been in childcare and celebrated them. They wore colorful t-shirts, emblazoned with the special needs logo, and they carried colorful balloons. This represented our theme —that they are the ones who bring the color to the world. It was a great evening and was an encouragement to all of us! We celebrated with cake and a variety of gluten-free desserts.

A few years later we came together to celebrate again. All of the volunteers, children, and their families were invited. Our senior pastor was the guest speaker for the evening. He thanked the volunteers and Bill and I, then gave a commitment to the families that special needs ministry would continue to be a vital and valued ministry in the church. The rest of the evening was spent celebrating what God had done!

The volunteers are the life-blood of the ministry. It cannot exist without them. Give thanks for them, appreciate them, and pray for them every day.

Chapter Eight

FAIRNESS

I AM A TEACHER. AT THE BEGINNING OF EACH SEPTEMBER, I welcome fifteen four- and five-year-olds to my classroom. During the year they will impact my life and hopefully, I will impact theirs.

When they walk through the door of my classroom, the first things I think about are *What do they need from me?* and *What is the challenge they are facing that I can help them with?* There will be the little boy that has so much energy and impulsive behavior that I will go home some days shaking my head, but I will also be smiling. There will be the little girl that lives inside her own imagination and doesn't know how to get out. There will be the child that has such a gift for math that I will have to figure out how to stay ahead of him. There will be the child that speaks so timidly and softly that I will not be able to hear him.

Webster's Dictionary defines fair as, *the state, condition, or quality of being fair, or free from bias or injustice; evenhandedness.* Somehow, somewhere, our society has corrupted this word and misunderstood it. Some believe that everyone needs to receive the same thing, or all people need to be exactly the same. In simple terms, if I give a child in my classroom a cookie, I need to give each of them a cookie. What about the child that has an allergy to gluten or sugar or fat? Is it fair to give that child a cookie?

As Richard Lavoie, a nationally known expert on learning disabilities, says in his DVD workshop, *How Difficult Can This Be?* "Fairness is not about giving people the same thing, it is about giving people what they need." I would give the child in my classroom with allergies something different. I would not treat them unjustly, but I would give him different things.

One time I was made aware of the children with special needs being denied a time of worship with *typical* children in the church, because some of them would lie on a bench instead of sitting on a colored square like the other children. Some volunteers felt this wasn't fair because then all of the children would want to sit on the bench. It is important to ask the question, "Should the child with special needs be encouraged to sit up and be more *typically* engaged in worship?" But it is also important to ask, "Is it acceptable if some children need something different in worship?" Can children who express worship differently be in the same room? All are equally valid questions. In our special needs ministry there are a variety of children with different abilities and needs. Worship is valid for all children whether they worship with their hands and feet in the air, headphones on their head, or their hands on the worship leader's guitar. They all need to experience worship, even if it looks different.

As a teacher I want to go back and apologize to so many people in the past. I know there will be even more in the future. Sometimes I have limited people and sometimes I have pushed them too hard. The one thing I have learned is that all people need to be treated with respect and grace, but the avenues through which those are delivered may be very different for each person. Realizing this truth has made me more adaptable as a teacher and more understanding as a friend.

One of the experiences I remember fondly was with my sweet friend and student, Ryan. Here is his story.

Every year I look forward to the parade of little people that will enter my classroom at the school where I teach. As we meet each other I only know a few facts about my students and they only know that I look like a grandma and I teach in "The Castle Room."

A few years ago a student walked into my classroom and captured my heart within moments. He was small in stature, but had a huge heart in that tiny little body! He blessed me and taught me so much that year.

Ryan made me face one of my challenges. I had a very hard time hearing him so I wore hearing aids the whole year (it helps when your husband is an audiologist!). I am so glad I did because I wouldn't want to have missed a thing he said!

During the year, I teach a unit on *"How to Be a Friend to Someone with a Disability"*[iii] based on *On A Roll For Jesus* by Joni Eareckson Tada. During the unit the children in my classroom earn money to send to Joni to refurbish a wheelchair for a child in another country that needs one. That particular year, the money was coming in rather slowly. I wondered if the kids understood and if the unit was meaningful to them. We moved on to our next unit and the kids and I prayed for the rest of the money.

Over the next couple of weeks, Ryan shared with me that he was going to have a garage sale. Each day he would mention someone new that had donated something. I really didn't think that much about it. Looking back on it, Ryan was so excited, and I wish that I had slowed down to pay more attention.

The morning of his garage sale, God woke me up. I jumped out of bed and told my husband Bill to wake up because we needed to go to a garage sale. I had an address and a subdivision but no map (for some reason I thought I could just find it). We drove around and ended up stopping at their neighborhood center to look at a map.

When we finally arrived at Ryan's house it was 10:30 a.m. The garage door was closed and there wasn't a sale in sight. As soon as I rang the doorbell I heard someone yell, "Mrs. Boggess is here! Mrs. Boggess is here!" When Ryan came to the door I asked him if he was still having a garage sale. He told me that he did have one but they had finished.

I said, "Well, do you have anything left? I would like to buy something."

Ryan immediately ran out the door and opened the garage door. There were all kinds of things on the floor. It looked like a garage sale that a five-year-old had set up. He had told me earlier in the week that he made some paintings for the garage sale, so I asked him if there were any left. Ryan showed me a couple and I fell in love with one and asked him if I could buy it. He said, "Yes" and I asked him how much it was. He told me it would cost ten cents.

I said, "Oh no, I think at least five dollars."

I turned to Bill and asked him if he had a five and as he pulled out a ten he said that was all he had. I handed Ryan the ten-dollar bill and he started to put it in his money bag and said, "There is no change."

I started laughing and said that was fine. I looked at his bag full of money and asked him what he was going to do with it.

Ryan looked up at me with such sincerity and said, "It is for the wheelchair, Mrs. Boggess. It is for the wheelchair!"

I started to cry and thanked him over and over again. What an incredible moment I will never forget! It had not occurred to me that Ryan's garage sale was to raise money for the wheelchair, yet here he was, continually thinking about it. He raised more than enough money to send to Joni and her ministry. His beautiful painting still hangs in my classroom.

While it is true that Ryan was a quiet little boy, he had a soft voice and it was high-pitched. The only thing Ryan needed from me was for me to hear him. Using hearing aids for a year was a small price to pay for not missing out on an incredible person. You see, the lesson for me is that Ryan wasn't the one with the weakness; rather, it was me. I needed to deal with my weakness. I have found this to be true so many different times in my life. When we see a child coming through the door of the church or a special needs classroom, we sometimes feel that we cannot accommodate their *weakness*. However, it is often our weakness that may need to be accommodated. Maybe it is hearing aids, patience, or just flexibility that we are lacking.

Now, let's take this a step further. Our own weakness can reveal itself in a variety of forms. There will be the adult in the church with political views so different from mine that I will avoid any mention of politics. There will be the adult that is so much smarter than I am that I will avoid deep theological conversations. There will be the person that has lived a lifestyle so different from mine that I will avoid sitting by him. There will be the adult that cannot speak with their voice that

I will avoid trying to communicate. Do I need to look at their weakness or mine before I address the issue of fairness?

As Richard Lavoie said, "Fairness is giving people what they need." If you have a child in your Sunday school class that needs to sit on a chair instead of the floor, let him. If you have a child that needs to worship with a loud voice, let him. It is okay for children to be treated differently based on their individual needs. Generally, *typical* children can accept others being treated differently based on their needs. They get it so much more than adults do. Don't let your *typical* children miss out on the blessing of being with children with special needs. They will adapt and will be the first ones to understand.

As for you, don't miss out on the adult with special needs who may walk through the doors of your church, either. His journey may be far different from yours. His appearance and abilities may look different from yours, but he is most likely the one through whom God wants to show you something. There are more handicaps in our society than the inability to walk or speak.

---

ii How Difficult Can This Be? The F.A.T. City Workshop, 1989. (DVD) Peter Rosen Productions, United States: Public Broadcasting Service.

iii On A Roll For Jesus Published in 2007 by Joni and Friends. Agoura Hills, CA. All Scripture is taken from the HOLY BIBLE, NIV ENCOURAGEMENT BIBLE (Published by Zondervan Publishing House, 2001)

~ 35 ~

Chapter Nine

FEAR VS. PITY

FOR MANY YEARS, MOST NEW VOLUNTEERS THAT CAME INTO the ministry came with a look of fear. They were afraid of the children with special needs, they were afraid of themselves, and they were afraid of hurting someone. So often we judge people that are afraid. Often times, however, people are afraid because they care so much. They don't want to hurt anyone and just need to be educated and given experience. No matter how seasoned we are, the feelings of fear can creep in.

I remember one Sunday morning when we had a visitor that surprised all of us. I thought we had experienced enough situations that we couldn't be surprised anymore until the day we met Toby. Toby was severely disfigured. It was hard for all of us to look at him and we felt guilty about it. We were stunned. We had so many questions about how to care for him and love him, but none of us could say a word.

Then, one of our volunteers walked up and embraced the family and then embraced Toby. She sat down beside him and started stroking his face over and over. Then she sang to him and prayed with him. It was the most beautiful thing I had ever seen. We were all stunned and tears started rolling down our cheeks.

I watched for an hour as the volunteer, Amy, was spellbound by Toby and continued to love on him until his parents came back to pick him up. After the family left, I went up to her and told her how beautiful it was. I said, "You didn't see his disfigurement or disability. You simply loved him. How did you do that?"

Amy responded back by saying that it was one of the hardest things she had ever done. She said, "I was praying the whole time. I couldn't do it on my own, but I wanted to love him the way Christ does." God melted her fears away by filling her heart with love.

In special needs ministry our first hurdle is often fear, and right on its heels is the emotion of pity. Pity must be overcome just as much as fear. Let me explain.

While I was on staff at our church, one year we emphasized the use of spiritual gifts with our volunteers. We had each volunteer take a spiritual gifts inventory and made sure they were using their gifts in the best way possible.

I don't know why it surprised me, but the volunteers in the special needs ministry were all very high in the gift of mercy. This makes sense and is easy to understand. What I learned, however, is that your greatest strength can also be your greatest weakness.

The best way to explain this is to share a story that my father once shared with me. My uncle's first wife had a severe mental illness. After she died he married a woman who had some physical challenges. One day my father was in Wichita Falls, where my uncle lived, and decided to visit my uncle and meet his new wife, Joanne. When my father entered the house, Joanne was sitting on a sofa across the room. My father went over to greet her and sat down on the sofa beside her. They all talked for a few minutes and after some time she offered my father a drink of water. He accepted, and then watched Joanne crawl off of the sofa and start crawling across the floor towards the kitchen. It greatly upset and embarrassed my father, who got up to go get the glass of water. My uncle reached out his hand and stopped my dad. He looked at my dad and said, "She has a handicap but you will be the one that disables her. Let her get the glass of water." Can it be true that a heart of mercy can disable someone?

At the time my father shared that story we had a little girl in our classroom that was affected by cerebral palsy and developmental delays. She would continually go over and open cabinets and pull everything out, so we had bought locks for the cabinet doors to keep her out. We were so proud that we had solved a problem in the classroom. The first Sunday after they were installed, the little girl's mother came in and asked what the locks were for. We told her that we put them on so that Lisa, her daughter, couldn't get into the cabinets anymore. The mother promptly told us that we needed to take them off. She said, "You aren't doing her any favors or me for that matter. Do you plan to lock everything up instead of teaching her 'No?'" Mercy, our greatest gift, was our greatest weakness. We were using mercy to hinder Lisa instead of empower her.

Unfortunately, it took us many years for this truth to really stick and we made mistakes with it over and over again and had to relearn it every time we had a new child or a new volunteer. Sweet little Carissa, affected by hydrocephalus, had to use a walker. She would often fall to the floor and grunt for something she wanted. All of our merciful volunteers would run to try to figure out what she wanted and would bring it to her hoping that was the desire of her heart.

This continued every Sunday morning until one day her mother peeked in to check on her daughter and watched the craziness that was going on. She said, "You do know that Carissa can talk don't you and that she can crawl or use the walker to get across the room, don't you?" Once again, our greatest gift, mercy, was also our greatest weakness. We all stopped getting Carissa what she wanted and cheered her on as she went herself to get what she desired. Every volunteer that followed would go to pick up what she wanted until we would say, "We love her enough to have her get it herself."

Many times in my life since then, I have been criticized, both in my private life and my ministry life, for not helping someone with a challenge. It is a hard balance to find, but I continually ask myself the question, "Will this help them or hurt them?"

Chapter Ten

SHUN, ENABLE OR EMPOWER

To be shunned—what a heartbreaking reality of our world. My most powerful memory of seeing someone shunned was with my grandmother. Before I was even born my grandmother had cancer of the larynx. She had an opening in her neck that she breathed out of, and because her vocal cords had been removed, she could only speak by pushing air through the hole in her neck. I loved Grandma Gossom, and have so many fond memories of baking with her in the kitchen and getting all dressed up as if we had somewhere fancy to go. I never thought of her as different from anyone else until we went shopping.

Grandma was a very friendly lady and absolutely loved children. She would go up to them at the store and start talking. Immediately the children would pull away from her and would often start crying. I never got used to how sad that made me feel. I ached for her. She wanted to express love to people and they would often shun her and walk away.

Enabling is such a buzzword in our society today. I see very little value in enabling anyone, whether they have special needs or not. Enabling lowers the bar, it disarms people, it causes depression and causes a person to be less than they are and who God has designed them to be. I have never seen it have a positive effect on a person's life.

Empowerment, on the other hand, makes everything possible. I know through my faith in Christ that God never enables me, but He consistently empowers me to do far more than I ever hoped or imagined.

Ten years ago, when my father was dying, I told God that I would do **whatever** He asked of me from that day forward no matter how much it scared me and no matter how difficult it was. At the time I was incredibly shy and self-conscious. I told God that even if He asked me to speak in public, I would do it.

Within two weeks I was asked to give a talk at a retreat. None of the people on the retreat committee had ever met me. It was crazy. What in the world did I have to say? But I knew that God wanted me to do it. I wish I could convey how unlikely a candidate I am to speak publicly and yet, God asked me to do it. Since then, I have spoken multitudes of times. God never enables me, but He does empower me.

I think the person that taught me the most about empowerment was my mother. First of all, my mother was always there for me as I was growing up, no matter what emotion I was experiencing. Quitting or believing I couldn't make it through something was not an option. She reminded me of my strengths, the trials I had previously overcome, and most importantly, the power available to me through my faith in God.

Throughout all the growing pains of life, I remember my mother always comforting me first, then stabilizing me, and lastly empowering me. In so many ways this reminds me of the course the special needs ministry has taken. In those early years of the ministry our main goal was to embrace and love the wounded. Families came to the special needs ministry with a similar experience; they had been rejected by a number of churches before they came through our doors. They were wounded, they were hurt, and to be honest, they expected us to hurt them again. Our only objective was to love them, welcome them, take care of their children and allow them to worship knowing that their child was well cared for. We had no idea that there were challenges we would face. We really had no idea what we were doing, but we knew that we needed to do it. We embraced them and we loved them.

Secondly, we tried to stabilize them. We attempted to stop the shaking, curb the fears, and stabilize them in the church. They needed to build relationships, have people love them and their children, and become comfortable in the church again. That takes trust and trust takes time.

In order to stabilize it is extremely important for the church not to pull the rug out from under these families. At various times we have faced some battles in protecting the special needs ministry. Not because anyone wanted to cause any harm, but because volunteers didn't understand the importance of stabilizing. Parents of children with special needs have to fight almost everywhere they go—at the doctor's office, the dentist's office, the school system, in neighborhoods, in grocery stores…the list never ends. The last place they should have to fight is in the church. I repeat: the last place they should have to fight is in the church!

Childcare should be available for women's ministry, men's ministry, and small group ministry. Families affected by special needs crave and need the stability of a church family and a group of people that are there to minister to them.

Lastly, there is no greater gift than empowerment. When we empower, we give a person hope, vision, and faith.

I truly do believe in empowering vs. enabling people. As I said before, one of the people that empowered me the most has been my mother. She never let me get away with thinking I couldn't do something or that something was too hard for me.

I will never forget when my oldest daughter was two and I started having gall bladder attacks. They were incredibly painful. I depended on friends and family to come stay with Bethany when I suffered attacks. When an ultrasound showed that I had over 200 gallstones in my gallbladder, it was obvious that I would have to have surgery right away.

This was my first surgery, except for the C-section I had. I was incredibly nervous. I will never forget Mom holding my hand as I was being wheeled into surgery. I looked up at Mom and said, "I can't do this. I can't, Mom." She looked me straight in the eye and said, "You don't have any choice, you have to do it. You will be fine." Mom gave me so much strength and I knew that I would be fine. I should mention this was before laparoscopic surgery was common, and before I had very many trials under my belt. I have to laugh now about how scared I was, but the point is, Mom gave me strength and still does to this day. Sometimes I think Mom wishes I would rely on her more but, "Mom, you raised me well! You have taught me to remain strong in a variety of situations."

Think about it. Think how much weaker we would all be if we hadn't faced difficult situations in our lives. Just as we want our children to stand on their own, we also want the children affected by disabilities to stand strong and be able to handle as much as they can. This is love—to empower people and give them the ability to face their challenges. Remember, people have real handicaps or challenges, but we could be the ones that disable them by limiting our expectations of them or their expectations of themselves.

Chapter Eleven

LISTENING WITH YOUR HEART

EARLY IN THE SPECIAL NEEDS MINISTRY A YOUNG MAN CAME along who had a number of physical challenges and a difficult time communicating orally. I will never forget the first time I met him and his mother. His mother said, "Now there is one thing you will have to do with William. You will have to listen with your heart." I knew that William had some challenges with his speech, but I didn't really know what she meant until I spent some time with him.

The first couple of Sundays, I couldn't understand William at all. I really tried to be patient and prayed that God would give me the ability to effectively communicate with him. I continued to pray and over time I was able to decipher William's speech.

I quickly learned that I had a number of areas in which I needed to listen with my heart. As I got to know William, I learned about all of the emotional challenges he had been through in the previous few years of his life. He needed me to listen with my heart when he acted up. He needed me to listen with my heart when he hit or kicked me. He was hurting so much inside and I needed to set aside all of the preconceived notions I had about communication. God needed to change my heart.

Over the years the lessons I learned through my friendship with William changed the way I looked at children with special needs and over time, the way I looked at all kids. So many of them are carrying a very heavy load and I will have to rely on my heart to understand why they are reacting the way they are.

Our youngest daughter, Sarah, has a tremendous ability to listen with her heart. For weeks I watched her sit by the bed of a loved one after a serious car accident. He couldn't speak for a variety of reasons, but Sarah always found a way to understand what was on his heart. She served him and loved him, and because of that, she could understand. I have also watched her do this with her precious five-year-old daughter. It is difficult for a five-year-old to share all of the emotions they feel, but I have been able to watch Sarah sit down beside her, with patience, to find out what was on her mind.

The ability to listen with your heart can come naturally, but it can also develop over time. I think this is one of the many reasons God asks us to serve one another. It gives us time, in the presence of another, to learn what they need and what they are going to be able to impart to us. Listen with your heart.

Chapter Twelve

WOOKIE WOOKIE

CALEB WAS ALL OF FIVE YEARS OLD. HE HAD SANDY BLOND hair and beautiful blue eyes. He was such a cute little boy and so full of life. I watched him from across the room thinking that I could just come into the classroom and we would instantly connect and be friends. Then I watched him raise his hands and turn them towards each other. He began to open and close each of his hands and repeatedly say, "Wookie Wookie." As I watched him, I thought I would ask him to stop and we would start talking together and get to know each other. No matter what I said, he continued to move his hands together and say "Wookie Wookie." I couldn't find a way to get him to do anything else. I listened to the words, "Wookie Wookie" for an entire hour. This went on for several weeks. I wanted to impact Caleb's life so much, but never seemed to be able to get past, "Wookie Wookie." One thing I have learned in ministry and life is, *when you try something repeatedly and it still doesn't work, it is time to do something else.*

So, one Sunday I came into the Sunday school room and saw Caleb walking around the room reciting names. It was a long list of names and at the end he said, "Tri-Star Pictures." We asked his dad when he came to pick him up what he was doing and he shared they had been to the movies the night before and Caleb was reciting the credits. I couldn't believe it! That night it hit me: *If he can memorize that well and that easily, he would be able to hide the Word of God in his heart without any problem.* I knew then what the something different would be the following week.

The following Sunday, I walked into the classroom and sat on the floor next to Caleb. I looked him in the eyes and held up my hands. I made my hands talk and say, "Wookie Wookie" again and again. Caleb looked at me, then my hands, and gave me an expression that said, "Hey, that's my gig." We played "Wookie Wookie" most of the hour. I had now entered his world and he was letting me in.

The next week I greeted Caleb with a "Wookie Wookie" and he responded back. After a few minutes in his world, I tried to get him to come into mine and he was receptive. I read a Scripture verse to him, pointed out the words as I did, and Caleb recited the verse. This is how our relationship started and how it continued. I always greeted Caleb with a "Wookie Wookie" and then we would learn Scripture together. He entered my world, but I had to first be willing to enter his. I continue to use this method as a teacher. If I have a child that is hard to reach I look for ways to enter their world, and then they may come into mine. As time goes on, I have realized how true this is for all people. If we greet them where they are first, it will be much easier to build a relationship with them later.

Chapter Thirteen

SHARING THE GOSPEL

ONE OF THE CHILDREN THAT CHANGED ME WAS A PRECIOUS little girl named Julia, the same name of my best friend in high school. The moment I met Julia, I fell in love with her. She was six years old, beautiful and happy and precious. In my mind she was one of God's angels sent here to teach all of us how to love. She taught us how to slow down, lie on the floor, and listen to soft music with her. She taught us to stop and pray. She taught me how to trust God.

There is an amazing volunteer that I haven't shared with you either. Her name is Heidi and she has served in the special needs ministry for about fourteen years now. She is a physical therapist, but that is not the only reason why she is so invaluable in our ministry. She is committed to the children and so passionate about serving them in the quietest and gentlest of ways. Over the years her passion has been to find a way to reach the hearts of the children we love. Heidi feels a deep responsibility to share the sacrificial love of Christ with them.

For years now I have had the image in my mind of Heidi kneeling before Christ in heaven and one by one, Christ presents the children she has served with whole and complete bodies. She hears their voices for the first time as each of them tells her the spiritual truths she taught them. Tears are running down her face as they individually thank her for introducing them to Christ, including Julia. At the end, the Lord kneels down to kiss her on the forehead and says,

"Well done, good and faithful servant! You have been faithful with a few things; I will put you in charge of many things. Come and share your master's happiness!"
Matthew 25:21 (NIV)

I am glad this is a constant burden on Heidi's heart and she is continually driven to find better methods to reach the children. She never stops researching and looking for better answers.

One of my favorite verses regarding evangelism is found in Colossians 4:2-6:

2 "Devote yourselves to prayer, being watchful and thankful. 3 And pray for us, too, that God may open a door for our message, so that we may proclaim the mystery of Christ, for which I am in chains. 4 Pray that I may proclaim it clearly, as I should. 5 Be wise in the way you act toward outsiders; make the most of every opportunity. 6 Let your conversation be always full of grace, seasoned with salt, so that you may know how to answer everyone." (NIV)

For me, this verse gives step-by-step instructions for evangelism in this ministry.

Not only do we need to pray, but we need to devote ourselves to prayer. This means an active choice and takes commitment.

Be watchful and look for opportunities.

Be thankful for the precious moments we have with people.

Pray that God will open a door in their hearts to the message of Christ. It may appear that they don't understand especially if they are non-verbal, but you never know what the Holy Spirit is doing.

Pray that we may share the gospel clearly. This is not necessarily researching the best methods with different disabilities. It can be praying for it and then letting go and trusting the Holy Spirit's intervention.

Be wise to outsiders. I never know what is going on in the mind and heart of a person or their family members. Remember everyone is carrying a heavy load so...

Be full of grace.

Be seasoned with salt.

So that we may be able to answer anyone, whether affected by blindness, deafness, physical challenges, intellectual challenges, or emotional challenges. God can give us exactly what we need to communicate with whomever we need to.

Colossians 4:2-6 gives me everything I need for evangelism. It provides step-by-step instructions. Then, Romans 10:17 reminds me to be filled with joy.

"Consequently, faith comes from hearing the message, and the message is heard through the word about Christ. But I ask: Did they not hear?
Of course they did."
Romans 10:17,18 (NIV)

Chapter Fourteen

LET'S BE HONEST

ON ONE PARTICULAR SUNDAY, AS A VOLUNTEER WALKED down the hall towards me, I recognized the expression on her face. I have had that expression before and so had many other volunteers. It was a look of shock, hurt, and disappointment. As I approached her I asked her what was wrong. I don't recall the specifics of what she shared, but I do recall how it affected me.

The volunteer shared that someone in the congregation had made some inappropriate remarks about one of our kids. She was stunned by it. I immediately sympathized with her feelings, but shared with her that all of us have people that we don't understand and we say the wrong things about them. We make assumptions and refuse to see them the way God does. I shared with her my own blind spot. As much as I love children with special needs, and as much as I love adults with special needs, there are some people that I cannot relate to and have blinders on about them. She was surprised by what I was saying and asked me to tell her more about my blind spots.

It wasn't easy for me to admit, but I shared with her that I have no understanding of people that are challenged by mental illness. I have no experience with people with mental illness and they scare me because they are unpredictable and I have no idea how to minister to them. If someone affected by schizophrenia came walking into the church and made a scene in the worship center, I would have no idea what to do. I would be afraid, and to be honest, I would be upset that they had interrupted the service. As open as I was trying to be, I had no idea what God had in store for me.

It was only two weeks later when one of the ushers came up to me and said they needed help downstairs with a young man who had come to church. I immediately assumed he had some physical challenges and they needed help. As we walked down the stairs to meet him, the usher shared that the young man was bipolar and schizophrenic. My heart both sank and started beating faster. My thoughts were racing. "I can't do this God! This is my biggest fear. You can't ask this of me. I have no idea what to do!" What could I do? I had already told God that I would do anything He asked of me.

As I approached the young man, my first assumption was that he was homeless. His appearance was ruffled and unkept. He smelled of tobacco and was very nervous. He paced back and forth, fidgeted with his hands, and couldn't be still. Luckily another children's ministry volunteer was with the young man and had made great headway in making him feel comfortable. As I approached I didn't know what else to do but sit down beside him, keeping some distance of course. For the purpose of this book, I will call him Michael. Michael immediately looked up at me, shifting his attention my way. He made a few sexually inappropriate comments and then started talking about the Bible.

I was nervous. I was scared, but I was also amazed by how much he knew about God's Word. He recited Scripture after Scripture to me, shared some of his church experience, and then some of his theology after years of studying. I was confused and fascinated by him.

Over the next several weeks, Michael returned to church and a ministry volunteer, my husband Bill, and I took turns being with him. We tried to show our love for him and figure out the best way to minister to him. Due to some inappropriate behaviors we decided it would be best if he were not left alone to wander around in the church. I remember during one of the services he put his head on my shoulder and cried like a baby throughout the entire service. Again, I was scared, yet full of compassion and bewilderment about how to minister to him. Little did I know how this experience would grow me in a new direction in ministry, and allow me to face my fears and learn to love him.

As the weeks progressed, I was continually amazed and blessed by Michael's knowledge of the Bible. At the same time, his unpredictable behaviors were increasing. He was approaching people for money and would become upset if he didn't get any. He was talking to different voices in his mind and was becoming increasingly nervous. I prayed for Michael and I prayed for myself. "Help me understand, Lord."

The last week I saw Michael, he came into the children's ministry area demanding to see me. As soon as I saw him, he looked me sternly in the eye, told me he was upset, and that we needed to talk. I glanced back at one of our leaders and asked him to tell Bill I would be in the prayer room with Michael and he could join us there. My fears were growing and I wanted someone to know where I was.

During that long walk down the hall I could tell by Michael's countenance that he was very hurt and upset. Apparently, he had realized that he was never left alone and he didn't like it. He shared that he felt a lack of trust. While we were in the prayer room that day he shared how hurt he felt and that the voices inside his head were getting louder and he couldn't take it anymore. In great detail he shared his plans to take his own life. I prayed with him, hugged him, and shared with him how much God loved him and could hear his prayers. I will never forget the next words he shared, "Do you know how much I don't want to be schizophrenic? I pray every day of my life that God will heal me."

It was then that I realized how much God had changed me. I was no longer afraid. I was no longer judgmental. I only felt compassion for my friend Michael. God brought someone into my life who would lead me to face my fears and help me confront one of my blind spots.

As Michael shared more details of his suicide plans, I told him that he needed help, help that I wasn't able to give him. He told me that he had used marijuana that week and had not taken his medications. He acknowledged he needed help.

I asked Michael's permission to bring in professionals and he agreed. Eventually a CIT (Crisis Intervention Trained) deputy was called, who took Michael to a mental health facility to get some medications and support. The police officers involved were amazing and extended compassion to Michael. Michael left relieved because he knew he was getting help and would be better soon.

I am changed from that experience. I will never be the same. I still have very little knowledge of or experience with mental illness, but I overcame some fears and let go of some previous assumptions I held. I saw my weakness and ignorance firsthand and it has allowed me to be a better leader and a better friend.

I have relived those weeks with Michael over and over in my mind. I have wondered what I should have done differently and how I could have ministered to him more. I have not seen Michael since then, and I have missed him. He changed me.

He caused me to be honest with myself and see my own sin, my own depravity, and the limits to my love. We all have people that are difficult to love and embrace, but once we do, we are one step closer to understanding God's love for us.

Chapter Fifteen

RECOGNIZING SIMILARITIES

I AM FIFTY-THREE YEARS OLD NOW. I HAVE WATCHED MYSELF grow up. I have raised two wonderful daughters and taught them at home for eleven years. I pour my heart and soul into my grandchildren. I have now taught a "bridge to kindergarten" class to 135 children. I have learned many valuable lessons from children along the way, but the lessons that have changed my perspective on life and people the most have come from the children we communicate as having "special needs."

The children I have met with special needs embrace life honestly. Most of the time their deficiencies are known. Most of the time they are honest when they are upset or frustrated. Most of the time their journeys are on display for everyone to see. Oftentimes they cannot hide their fears or hurts, or at least they don't work so hard to hide them the way the rest of us do. Through them I have learned to meet people where they are, to look at the person God created and not who He didn't create, and to expect the unexpected.

So many of the children Bill and I worked with had unexpected challenges on a regular basis in all areas of their life such as medical, educational, social, emotional and spiritual. Not only have the children had to walk this journey but so have their parents and siblings. Expecting the unexpected often becomes a way of life.

There are a few of us that will have life turn out pretty much the way we expected, at least for a while. Then there are those of us, and I would venture to say most of us, that have many changes of course during our journey. Some of those changes are rather "serendipitous," or an unexpected surprise, while others may cause a great deal of confusion, doubt, fear, and even pain. My journey has changed courses many times throughout my life and over time I have gone through feelings of fear, shock, loneliness, grief, anger, and helplessness.

What intrigues me is that we all tend to think that we are the only ones this has happened to. We are the only ones that have lost a dream or are left stunned and bewildered after an unexpected event.

Quite often I have had a parent of a special needs child tell me that parents without children with special needs don't understand how hard it is, day in and day out with the loneliness, the disappointment, the strain on the marriage, and the stress of not knowing what to do when something unexpected occurs. I understand why they feel that way, but as I have aged and gained more life experience, it seems in reality that we all have more in common than we care to admit. I have met very few people that have not experienced deep sorrow and disappointment, and, if I think they haven't, they probably haven't shared the deep wounds of their heart, or they haven't had their turn yet. We are a fallen people in a fallen world, great sorrow is everywhere and no one is exempt from it.

I will never forget January 14, 2001. I had spent the morning with my mother and my brother in a surgery waiting room. My father was having a growth removed from his esophagus. He had trouble swallowing and had choked a number of times. Doctors found the growth in his esophagus and were concerned that it may be malignant. Just the thought of anything happening to my dad was difficult for me to even think about. He was my hero.

During the surgery my family received a phone call that my grandfather was very ill and was not expected to live through the day. My mother's brothers felt that she should head to Wichita Falls immediately to be with him. She shared that my father was still in surgery and she needed to wait until he was out of recovery before she could even think about leaving. I told her that I could stay with Dad and take him home and care for him if she felt she needed to leave. After Dad was out of surgery and recovery, Mom decided that she would head up to be with her father the next day and I would stay with Dad until she got back.

Plans were made and we thought we knew the course of the week. I left the hospital to go pick up Bill at work. As I was waiting for Bill, I was thanking God for getting my father through the surgery and was lifting my grandfather up in prayer, when the phone rang. It was Bill's brother on the phone, crying. I was stunned as I listened to what he told me. Tears were filling my eyes as Bill walked out to greet me. How could I tell him that in the last thirty minutes his father and nephew had been in a tragic car accident and they didn't expect his father to live? Our journey was taking a different course… once again.

It was a long silent drive home. We were both trying to process all that had happened that day and were wondering what was ahead of us. We decided to leave our children in the care of some friends while we mechanically packed our suitcases. We decided that Bill, his brother and his sister-in-law would leave on the earliest flight they could get. I would pack for our children and my niece and we would fly out as soon as we could the next day.

As we were packing, the phone rang again and we heard the words we never wanted to hear: Bill's father had passed away. Apparently a teenager had dropped a cell phone while driving and leaned over to pick it up. He ran a red light and hit my father-in-law's car. This small decision took my father-in-law's life and severely scarred my nephew's.

Disappointment, disbelief, anger and overwhelming loss—our world had changed forever. Over the next year I watched my children start to question God and face the harsh realities of life. My oldest daughter suffered a huge heartache. In the last conversation she had with my father-in-law, she had shared her faith with him and he yelled at her. We didn't know about this hurt until a year later.

Soon after the loss of my father-in-law, my maternal grandmother and grandfather died, and less than two years later, I saw my beloved daddy start to fade before my eyes. I just never thought it was possible that I could actually lose my dad. Another year later and my brother-in-law died as a result of diabetes complications.

During that time in my life, I was mechanically walking around with a bruised and broken heart, still trying to meet the needs of people depending on me. Some Sundays I felt like I could barely function. Yet, on numerous Sundays someone would come to me complaining about the ministry. We needed to be doing this or that. We were failing at something else. We should have handled something differently.

People didn't really know the wounded battleground of my heart, mostly because I didn't let them see it. There have been many battles since then and most often, I kept them close to my heart. What I have learned in the process, however, is that none of us knows the extent of the wounded hearts that walk in and out the doors of the church. We live in a fallen world, full of fallen expectations.

I have always been curious about heaven. Even though I am anxious to know what it is like, I am glad God keeps it a secret. It will be a wonderful surprise one day! I do wonder, however, if God is going to reveal to us that the people we thought had a challenge, or more honestly a deficit, were really the ones that were handling life the best way and were closer to God in the process. For example, I think of sweet Julia. She may be having amazing fellowship with God in her silence. I think of Jacob, deaf and blind, but honestly, has the sweetest form of worship I have ever seen. I think of Hilary. She never questions living out her faith or who she loves…she just does.

Chapter Sixteen

ADVOCATE VS. INFLUENCE

ONE EVENING GOD KEPT WAKING ME UP ALL NIGHT. Forgive me, Lord, but I get agitated when you do that! I kept trying to ignore Him until I couldn't anymore and I got out of bed. God was telling me that I needed to go to a meeting the next morning.

I got up, got ready for church, and told Bill that God told me to go to a meeting after church and I had no idea why. I didn't want to go and I felt like I was just plain too busy. I had received an email a couple of weeks prior from a pastor's wife, inviting me to a coffee about mentoring. I have always been fascinated by the whole concept of mentoring, but had no way of fitting it into my life. But God told me to go anyway.

The meeting was held in a beautiful home. I walked in and was given some papers to fill out. I robotically filled them out, but left much of the questionnaire blank because I had absolutely *no idea why I was there*!

We were asked to go around the room and share our name and if we wanted to be a mentee or a mentor. When it was my turn I said, "I am Deana Boggess," giggled, and said, "I have no idea why I am here, but I am here." (What a way to make friends and influence people!)

The person sitting next to me looked at me and said, "You are Deana Boggess? *The* Deana Boggess?" I said, "Yes, uh, I guess so." The woman looked back at me with tears in her eyes and said, "I am in church because of you." She then started sharing her story with me.

She had a daughter with Down Syndrome and had heard about the special needs program and had started coming to the church. When I hear things like this I just fall on the floor and say, "This has absolutely nothing to do with me and EVERYTHING to do with God."

I thanked her for her kind words, and soon after, my husband dropped by, needing something. I handed the paperwork off and said I needed to go. On the way out the door, I thought my being there was all about that conversation and told God to do whatever He needed to do.

About ten days later, it dawned on me that this was the evening for mentees and mentors to meet. I hadn't heard anything else about it, but felt God prompting me to check on where things were left. I may be clueless about a lot of things, but I never like to let anyone down!

I called the woman in charge, who said, "Didn't you get the email? You will be mentoring April." (This was the same woman from the meeting, with tears in her eyes.) By this time it felt way too divine to not accept the appointment. I went to the meeting and April and I hugged, cried, and made plans to meet. As I hugged her I thought, "Okay God, I still don't have any time, but I told you I would do whatever you asked of me."

I truly don't know the forms of these words, but you don't have to be a mentor to be a mentor, nor do you have to be a mentee to be a mentee. In other words, April offered me as much or more as I offered her.

It quickly became apparent to us what God wanted to accomplish. April was in the battle of her life to get services for her daughter and I was there to show her how to advocate with grace, or how to influence. The lesson in it for me was to say, "Yes, God, I will do what you want" and then watch Him do it.

April and I met for the next three months. It was powerful for both of us in different ways. God laid everything out for me. Every week I would sit down at the computer and God would show me the direction of the discussion for that week. We studied the life and philosophy of the ministry of Billy Graham, who was a mentor to one of my mentors during my twenties.

I am not sure I know everything those three months did for April, but I do know what they did for me. I developed a better understanding of the difference between advocating and influencing, and when to use each one.

Advocating conjures up picket signs in my mind. It is protesting. It is fighting for someone or something. It is doing what you need to do to make change. If given the opportunity, I would have held many picket signs over the years. My favorite phrases would have been *Stop It!* or *Get Up and Do Something About IT!* There would not have been much grace, but a feisty, narrow-minded housewife fighting for something she believed in. Let me just say, I am only including myself in this image of advocacy.

Advocacy is wonderful and powerful and life-changing. My dad was an advocate and I saw him make a lot of positive changes in the world. It is necessary in our society. It is why we have the freedoms we do. It is why fewer people are discriminated against. It is why fewer groups of people are marginalized in our society. I am all for advocacy!

On the other hand, sometimes we need to take down our picket signs and merely influence. For example, remember Michael, the young man suffering from mental illness? Would I have changed more from listening to a group of protestors fighting for the rights of the mentally ill, or by having Michael in my life for those few weeks? I remember very few protests, but I will never forget Michael.

I have the opportunity to influence every waking moment of my life. Influence happens when I send an email to the elders of the church sharing what God is doing in the special needs ministry. Influence happens when I introduce one of the children with special needs to one of the pastors of the church. Influence happens when I introduce a child with special needs to their peers on the playground. It happens when I have pictures around the church of these precious children, when stories are shared from the pulpit, and when youth are invited to serve in the ministry and help change the culture of the church. Advocacy has its place and time for effectiveness, but given at the wrong time it can cause defensiveness and a church to feel backed into a corner. Influence, however, at the right time, can cause people to be gently touched in a way that changes their perspective.

Chapter Seventeen

UNEXPECTED TOOLS

THERE ARE SO MANY THINGS I LOVE ABOUT GOD, BUT ONE OF the things I love the most is how He uses our weaknesses and our struggles to accomplish great things. Over the years, Bill and I have served alongside a great person, a man named David. We first met David about fifteen years ago while he was serving in children's ministry as a kindergarten teacher. I was always impressed by his gracious control of a classroom and the love he had for all children. He is such a man of God and has so much wisdom and grace.

When we all started serving together in special needs ministry, we were all floundering together. We have had many ups and downs in ministry, but we were all very committed and trusted God to cover in every way that we were lacking.

One of the many things I have appreciated about David is that he has always held us accountable. He reminded us to not hold onto the ministry too tight, and to empower others to grow and serve. He also reminded us to not feel guilty when we couldn't do it all. This was probably the biggest area of struggle for me. No matter how much we did, I continually felt guilty about what we didn't do. There was always another family that needed acceptance and love. There was always another child that needed to know they were loved and we simply couldn't do it all. David helped us keep perspective.

David also reminded us to attend worship. There were so many Sundays that we were short-staffed, or we would be leaving for worship and a couple would come up to us with tears in their eyes because they had just received a diagnosis that their child was autistic. David wouldn't let us serve two hours and miss church. I have to admit that sometimes it was frustrating because I wanted to try to meet every need. I am so glad that he cared about our spiritual well-being because ultimately, that was best for the ministry as well.

We have grown to love David and his wife, Kathy, over the years. I will never forget one evening when we were over at their house visiting. The tone of the evening changed suddenly at one point, and Kathy shared with me that David had been diagnosed with Parkinson's disease. For several weeks I had been concerned about him because he didn't seem as strong as he used to be. When Kathy shared the diagnosis with me I got tears in my eyes. David would no longer be just one of the volunteers, but he would also be one of the ones we would eventually serve.

It has been a difficult and humbling road for David. 2 Corinthians 12:11 is one of my favorite verses. *For when I am weak, then I am strong.* It would only be a matter of time before God would reveal His power in David's new weakness.

We had a new young man come into the ministry who suffered from severe autism. Whenever he would get upset, he would bang his head on the floor repeatedly. We tried everything we could think of to calm him but nothing worked. He would only bang his head harder and longer.

One day I walked into the special needs classroom and this young man was lying on the floor. David was kneeling beside him and had his hand on the young man's chest. David looked up at me and said, "This is one of the ways that God is using my Parkinson's disease." Apparently the tremor in David's hand was calming to the young man. All he had to do was rest his hand on the young man's chest and he would calm down. It was amazing to me that this worked, and amazing that David was letting God use his disability to minister to this young man. What a great way for God's power to be demonstrated in his weakness. Now, a few years later, he has had the beautiful blessing of using it to calm his newborn granddaughter.

There are many unexpected tools to be used in special needs ministry. One of the things I admire the most about David and Bill is they have the uncanny ability to quickly look over a situation with a child and recognize the tools available to them. It can be a teen helper, a leader in the hallway that the child connects with, deep pressure techniques, calming techniques, or even a grasshopper on the wall (I have actually seen that used!). Some of the ability comes from intuitiveness, some from experience, and some from relying on the Holy Spirit. God will give you the tools you need, you just have to look for them and accept them.

Chapter Eighteen

UNEXPECTED MENTORS

I WAS AT A WOMEN'S BIBLE STUDY AND WAS ON MY WAY TO PICK up
my children when I noticed a very intriguing lady. I couldn't tell how
old she was, but it did appear that she had some intellectual challenges.
I watched her for a few minutes as she was interacting with moms
coming to pick up their children. Her name was Hilary, and she was
apparently the teacher for a classroom of toddlers. Everyone talked to
her with such respect and thanked her for taking care of their children.
None of them seemed to care at all about her intellectual challenges
and they were all grateful that they had someone as incredible as Hilary
watching their children. I was amazed at how great she was with children and couldn't take my eyes off of her. Finally I went up and introduced myself. She was very relaxed and hospitable. For the next couple
of weeks we chatted off and on until finally Hilary asked if I would like
to have lunch with her. I gladly accepted and was happy to have plans
since it was also my birthday.

We went to a nearby restaurant and ordered lunch. I started to pay
for our meals and she stopped me and said, "No, this is on me. It is
your birthday." I said, "No, you don't need to do that." We argued
back and forth and then she put her hand on mine and said, "Don't
you understand how important this is to me?" It was hard, but I knew
that I needed to let her pay for the meal.

I wasn't really sure what to talk about, but decided to ask her about
serving in the nursery. I told her that a lot of people looked up to her.

She shared with me about how much she enjoys children and how comfortable she is with them. Then she said, "But I am not really doing what I want to do." I asked her what she wanted to do and she said that she wanted to be able to tell the stories of Jesus to children. She said that she knew the stories, but no one ever lets her tell them. I was shocked and moved by what she said.

I spoke with a couple of people that week and we made arrangements for her to start teaching on Sunday morning. She loved it! Over the years, Hilary became more and more connected to the church. She began doing some office work for the church, had babysitting jobs, taught during childcare, and served in the AWANA (Approved Workmen Are Not Ashamed) Bible program as a leader.

My lunch with Hilary provided a great opportunity for me. For the next nine years, Hilary and I met for Bible study and accountability. I had no idea how to mentor Hilary, but she was well equipped to mentor me. We used a variety of materials throughout those years. Some worked well and others didn't at all. I remember I bought one children's Bible study program and was excited about using it. The second week of the study Hilary started crying. She was afraid to tell me and was especially afraid of letting me down. She looked at me with tears in her eyes and said, "Mrs. Boggess, I am a special needs person and this is way too hard for me." We hugged, we cried and we prayed together. This was my first lesson from Hilary. Don't be afraid to be humble and vulnerable. Be honest about where you are spiritually.

My love and appreciation for Hilary grew over the years. We had fun together talking and laughing. Sometimes we would simply drive around in the car singing songs and talking with the heaviest Southern accent we could muster. We also spent a lot of time exploring some of Hilary's favorite stores, like dollar stores and craft stores.

I never had an encounter with Hilary, however, that didn't teach me something. Intellectually, Hilary is blessed with eternal youth. Spiritually, she is well beyond her years. There is a reason that Scripture tells us to come to God with the faith of a child.

One hot summer day, Hilary and I stopped by a sandwich shop for lunch. We had some nice conversation, but the whole time I was distracted watching a woman having lunch with her son. Her son had the blessing of Down Syndrome. I wanted to go up and talk to them and share with them about the special needs ministry at our church, yet I just wasn't sure what to say. I didn't say anything to Hilary about it until I got in the car.

As we were preparing to head back to church and I looked over at Hilary and shared with her that I couldn't get them off of my mind. I told her that I wanted to introduce myself and tell them about the ministry, but I didn't know where to start.

Hilary looked over at me, and with a firm voice said, "Mrs. Boggess, if God is laying it on your heart to talk to them, then that is what you need to do!" I started to make excuses and Hilary looked at me and said, "I am not putting on my seatbelt and we are not leaving until you do!"

I turned the car off and said, "Okay, you are right. I will go talk to them, but you come with me." Hilary confidently looked at me and said, "Oh no, this is God's deal for you, not for me. I will wait right here." I had a great conversation with the mom and her son. That experience was probably about my needing to grow in reaching out to people. I am glad to say, however, that I did see the mom and her son in church about a year later. I laugh about that day every time I think about it. To this day, Hilary doesn't let me get away with anything. She faithfully prays for me, challenges me, and holds me accountable.

It breaks my heart that Hilary and I no longer meet on a regular basis. I truly miss her and I miss the spiritual impact she had on my life. I know it has been hard for her to understand the demands on my time, but she still loves me, prays for me, and sharpens my perspective whenever she can.

I often seek people out to mentor me and at times, I have even whined that I didn't have someone in my life to fill that role. At fifty, however, I now realize that mentors are all around me, I just need to pay attention.

Eight years ago I was on staff at our church as a preschool coach and special needs director. I had home schooled for ten years, and now my oldest daughter was in public high school and my youngest daughter was in the next building attending our church school. My oldest daughter was starting to struggle with her faith and was starting to challenge everything that was familiar to her, but she was also serving as a mentor to me.

One day I had a knock on the door and a young man asked if he could talk to me. He shared that he was concerned about my daughter, Bethany, and wanted to share some things with me. My heart instantly sank. I was afraid of what I might hear.

He shared his heart out of concern for Bethany and I know it was difficult for him, but I will never forget the words, "Your daughter is hanging out with despicable homeless people."

Two thoughts instantly flashed through my mind. *Is she safe?* and *What kind of situation is she in?* The momma in me always comes out first! Within seconds, though, I was saddened by his use of the word *despicable* when referring to homeless people. I looked at the young man and said I was glad that he came and shared his concern with me, but I might be more concerned with his use of the word *despicable*.

I went home that night and asked Bethany about what I'd been told. She told me that she did spend time with homeless people. She told me about two men that live downtown who are homeless and deaf. They have no one to talk to and she knows how to communicate with them, so why shouldn't she? "Isn't that what Jesus would do, Mom?" I really didn't know how to argue with that.

To be honest, Bethany wasn't as careful as she probably should have been and the young man was looking out for her. She still needed to grow in discernment and wisdom, but as a Christian, I needed to appreciate her ability to embrace people in a variety of situations.

Over the last eight years, I have learned many things from my precious daughter. She has challenged me to love all people. She has challenged me to take my faith more seriously. She has challenged me to live more simply.

Because of Bethany, I have had the blessing of hanging out with circus people, people with tattoos, piercings, dreadlocks, and even chickens in their kitchen, and I am richer for it. Jesus didn't set margins on those He loved; He just loved.

I admire and look up to Bethany for so many reasons. God has an amazing daughter in her and I cannot wait to see what all is going to happen in her life. She is determined, strong, adventurous, and incredibly compassionate. She never struggles with the materialism of this world. If she has food, shelter, and clothes on her back, she is content. If you receive a gift from her, you can be assured that a great deal of thought and love went into it.

Thank you, sweet Bethany, for not giving up on this old lady! You have broadened and colored my world in a multitude of ways! You have been a fabulous mentor for me!

Chapter Nineteen

TEACHING *TYPICAL* CHILDREN ABOUT CHILDREN WITH SPECIAL NEEDS

IT HAS BECOME A HIGHLIGHT OF MY LIFE TO TEACH *typical children* about children with special needs. I love watching them go through a metamorphosis. You can see it so clearly (it is a little messier with adults!).

I teach a *bridge class* for a private preschool. It is a class for children that may have missed the age cut off for entering kindergarten or their parents feel they need another year for one reason or another. I feel as though this class was specifically designed for me, because it offers me the opportunity to do the things I love and care about the most. I am able to teach children how to read, teach them about Jesus and His love for them, develop in them a love for learning and exploring, and answer some of the questions in their minds that seldom get answered. Children are incredibly open to children with challenges. It is often the adults who build up the walls. Usually, children just want their questions answered.

I try to help my students understand that we all have challenges and we all have gifts given to us by God. My hope is that they hear this message all year long, but I do devote a month of my year to specifically teaching them about disabilities.

At the beginning of the month it always feels a little uncomfortable. Even though I have done it for seven years now, I always ask myself the same questions. Will they understand? Will it be too much for them to handle? How will the parents respond? Should I make the unit shorter? Should I make it longer? Every year, however, I am continually amazed at the impact it makes on children as well as their parents.

My favorite verse for this unit is:

"That is why, for Christ's sake, I delight in weakness…For when I am weak, I am strong."
2 Corinthians 12:10 (NIV)

I love the way Christ used parables to teach us spiritual truth. I think God uses oxymorons to teach us truth. *For when I am weak, I am strong.* I think if we could all understand the truth behind that Scripture, the world would be a different place. God has changed me tremendously over the last ten years, but one of the biggest ways is in my understanding of this concept. I am weak in so many areas of my life, but I can see how much God's power is demonstrated when I embrace those weaknesses. For example, I do not consider myself a gifted writer; however, I believe that God has asked me to write this book and my writing abilities (or disabilities) are no obstacle for Him. As long as I am willing, God is certainly able. If I can get this across to children, and consequently their parents, the sky will be the limit in their lives, and the ripple effect of that is mind blowing!

During the month of our unit on disabilities, I devote a week each to the physically disabled, the blind, the deaf or hearing impaired, and the mentally and intellectually impaired. I use a curriculum developed by Joni Eareckson Tada called, *On a Roll for Jesus!*[iv] for my framework, then add people and experiences from my life to supplement the unit. One of Joni's ministries is *Wheels for the World*. This ministry collects wheelchairs, takes them to correctional institutions for refurbishing, and then redistributes them around the world to individuals who need, but cannot afford, a wheelchair. Many of the people this ministry serves have lived a life of isolation because they are immobile.

As I mentioned earlier in this book, Joni Eareckson Tada was a young healthy girl who, at age seventeen, dove into shallow water and suffered a severed spinal cord as a result of the accident. She has been a quadriplegic ever since she was seventeen. I can only imagine how difficult the journey has been for her, but the incredible miracle has been how God has used this tragedy to reach the world. Joni has been an advocate for those affected by disabilities, has spoken before many presidents, has served on the National Council on Disability under President Reagan and President Bush, and the Disability Advisory Committee to the U.S. State Department under Secretary of State Condoleezza Rice. She founded the International Disability Center in California and holds many honors and awards. Joni Eareckson Tada personifies *When I am weak, then I am strong.*

Joni has been one of my heroes since I was a young teenager and now she has become a hero for over one hundred five-year-olds. Each Monday throughout our unit on disabilities, I show the children a segment of a DVD created by Joni. The children quickly think of her as one of their close friends, and at the end of the DVD, they applaud. Last year one of my students asked if Joni could hear us clapping for her. She is real to them and they love her.

As with the volunteers that serve in our ministry, my first objective with this unit is to start to break down the wall of fear. I don't know about you, but I remember as a child being taught that it was impolite to stare at someone with a disability. This is absolutely true; however, this indirectly teaches children to not communicate at all with someone that has a disability. My objective is to help my students see the person first, not the wheelchair, or cane, or hearing aids. Thus, every year, my assistant is a wheelchair. If I can break down the fear and discomfort associated with a wheelchair, I have broken down a big chunk of the wall.

On the first day of our unit, I don't say anything about the wheelchair; I just have it next to my teaching chair. Children will ask me why it is there and by the end of the day a couple of children have touched it.

On the second day, I ask if anyone would like to sit in it. I don't believe I have ever had a child sit in it on the second day. On the third day I ask my *line leader* if he or she would like a ride to the lunchroom. Invariably, the first line leader does not want to ride in the wheelchair.

By the fourth day, ninety percent of the children are fighting to ride in the wheelchair and pop wheelies with me down the hallway. A HUGE chunk of the wall has come down now, just because they are no longer afraid of the wheelchair. They now think it is cool and FUN. This unit has evolved each year and has hopefully become clearer and more meaningful for my students.

Throughout this unit the children will also be involved in raising money for a wheelchair to be refurbished and distributed to a child in another country. Remember my story of Ryan and his garage sale? Out of my fifteen students, I typically have about five of them go above and beyond and come up with a brilliant idea and raise quite a bit of money for the wheelchair. I will have about five children meet the minimum and another five who won't participate. Watching the top five children raise money is one of the huge blessings of my life. I will have the opportunity to watch their hearts change and grow and their little faces get excited with every additional dollar they earn. Every year I encourage the parents to not let their children miss it. The harder they work, the more blessed they will be.

One year I realized that I have gone about this all wrong in the past. I needed to help the *parents* get it first. So, I held a meeting for the parents and showed them Joni's first DVD so they could understand what her ministry is all about. Then I gave them an outline of the unit. Next I explained The Butterfly Effect or the Ripple Effect of what the children will be able to accomplish. We spent some time brainstorming about how their children could earn the money and how they could make this meaningful for their children. I did not execute that meeting very well, but God still had it covered.

Over the next several weeks, parents and children had dinner table discussions on how the children were going to raise money. I kept my hands off of the fundraising efforts and focused on the lessons on disabilities.

I shared Andy Andrews' book, *The Boy Who Changed the World*, with the kids. The story shares about how one person's contribution can change the world. BUT, there was someone before them that impacted them, and there was someone before them that they were changed by. I had no idea that the wheels were already turning in those five-year-old minds. They already had amazing ideas for how they were going to raise enough money for a wheelchair.

One night during the unit, in the middle of the night, God suggested to me that for every dollar that was raised, I should post a butterfly on the wall of the castle in my classroom. The children had come up with amazing ideas on how to raise money and the money started steadily coming in. Within a week, the castle wall was covered and we had run out of room. The director of our school suggested that we move the butterflies to the hallways of the school. Butterfly production increased and my wonderful aide and I could not keep up. Parents started making butterflies at night. Staff started making butterflies. My family members started making them. Pretty soon, one side of the hallway had a stream of butterflies down it, then the other side was covered, then a lunchroom, the entry way, and lastly another lunchroom. The Butterfly Effect kept spreading[v]. I would walk down the hallway of the school and parents and board members would hand me checks to add to the total. The excitement added to the kids' commitment and sacrifice. I stopped telling the children how many wheelchairs they had raised after ten. The final number would be revealed at the celebration on the last day.

For that day, our room mother had bought enough balloons to represent the number of wheelchairs we had enough money for. Another mother had made a beautiful cake, and another mother had arranged a beautiful surprise that I was totally unprepared for. We anxiously gathered in the lunchroom with parents, family members, friends, and the director of the school to celebrate. As I walked into the lunchroom I saw my sweet hero, Joni, on a computer screen. I thought one of the mothers had decided to show another DVD clip to the children. Then I realized that Joni was *talking to me*. She was Skyping with us! I will never, ever forget those precious moments with her. What an honor and a privilege! Joni stayed with us as long as she could. I took her out in the hall to let her know how much money had been raised. I needed to keep the suspense for the kids a little bit longer than she could be with us.

After my chat with Joni, I had all of the kids come up front, and with great excitement I handed out fifteen balloons—one for each child, and each balloon represented one wheelchair. We all clapped and marveled over what God had done. Then, a good friend of mine, Jabe, shared his testimony with us. Jabe is ten years old and is affected by spina bifida. He showed pictures of all of the amazing things he has been able to do in spite of his inability to walk. He also shared how dear to his heart God is. It was great for the kids to be able to see the power of God and God's strength through Jabe's "weakness."

The celebration continued as I brought out one...two...three...four...five more balloons! The children had raised over $3,000 and had enough money to refurbish and distribute **20** wheelchairs. None of us will ever be the same!!

It isn't only in the educational classroom that we can teach *typical children* about children with special needs. The Sunday school class is also a great venue.

A number of years ago, we had a child come to our church that was born without eyeballs. Yes, he appeared different and yes, children would stare. They may have thought it was safe to stare, because Charley couldn't see. Charley knows when people are staring, though. It doesn't take eyesight to know that people are staring at you, but the beautiful thing about Charley is that he didn't let it stop him. It made a better him!

At first, Bill and I weren't sure what to do for Charley. We wanted to make sure that Charley would feel loved and welcomed in our church family, so Bill and Charley's parents and teachers talked about it and decided to be very upfront about it.

On Charley's first Sunday in the classroom, his teachers had him come to the front of the class and the teachers shared about Charley's physical challenge. They shared that Charley gets to know people by feeling their faces and they asked if anyone would like to come up and meet Charley. Gradually the whole class came forward and Charley went down the line feeling the children's faces. One of the children in particular felt an immediate bond with Charley and became his peer buddy. During that hour, the children asked questions and they were answered either by Charley or the teachers. They simply needed their questions answered, and with Charley's charisma and spiritual maturity, it didn't take long for him to become a favorite in Sunday school!

One of my favorite accounts of answering a child's questions occurred on the playground one day. Bill had taken one of the children Jacob, outside to get some fresh air. Jacob has Trisomy 13. He is in a wheelchair and is legally blind and deaf.

As Bill was walking around with Jacob, he noticed a little boy staring at Jacob. Bill quickly introduced Jacob to the little boy. The little boy asked Bill what was wrong with Jacob. Bill explained that he was missing a chromosome and this made it difficult for Jacob to walk. The little boy just stood there listening. Soon, another little boy came up. The first little boy just looked at him and matter-of-factly said, "This is Jacob. He is missing a chromosome. He likes to play like we do." The little boy nodded his head and both of them ran off to play.

That was truly a teachable moment, and they happen all day long. Just as my father walked the road with me and taught me, all of us can do the same. It is along the road that children will begin to understand. They are watching when I am at the grocery store and greet someone with a disability. They are listening to how I talk about people. They will touch people the way I touch them.

[iv] Andrews, A. (2000) The Boy Who Changed the World. New York, NY: Publishers, Inc.

[v] Andrews, A. (2010) The Butterfly Effect. Thomas Nelson, Inc.

Chapter Twenty

THE DISAPPEARING MINISTRY

AFTER THE NEW BUILDING AT HILL COUNTRY BIBLE CHURCH was completed and our wonderful classroom was decorated and moved into, we called for an evaluation. We asked my dad to come and give an honest evaluation of the facilities and the ministry. We wanted to know if we were meeting the basics needs of the special needs community and how we could improve and be able to go above and beyond.

Dad had now gone back into ministry after retiring from the Equal Employment Opportunity Commission. He was serving as a pastor for a small country church, so when he came into our brand new facility that could accommodate 5,000 people, he was over-whelmed. We had the blessings of people, finances, and facilities. Dad shared that the majority of the work was done because the building had to meet current accessibility codes in correlation with the Americans with Disabilities Act. The doorways, restrooms and water foun-tains accommodated wheelchairs, and we were already meeting reason-able accommodations for a worship facility.

One of the first issues he brought up, however, was the vastness of the worship center, as well as the rest of the campus. Due to the size of the campus, it would be a great deal of territory for a well-abled person to navigate, let alone a person with physical challenges. My fa-ther himself had challenges with walking the campus, so it was easy to see that this was an important issue. It was troublesome not only for people with challenges to their legs, but people who may be struggling with cancer and other debilitating diseases. The vastness of the space could also be a hindrance to a family with a child with emotional or behavioral challenges. It took only one conversation with our facilities pastor and the number of handicapped parking spaces was increased and benches were added throughout the campus so people could sit down and rest.

Dad commented on the Braille signage throughout the building that blended into the facility and then made a few more suggestions, such as large print Bibles, large print bulletins, hearing devices and wheelchairs that could be used by guests.

Before he left, he made a comment that really stayed with Bill and me. He said, "You will know your ministry is successful when you can't see it anymore. It should be in the very fabric of your church." We were stunned by his comment at the time, and had no idea what it meant. Dad shared some of his thoughts on this with us, but it wasn't long before Dad was diagnosed with multiple myeloma cancer and died just nine days after his diagnosis. So many times I have wanted to talk further with dad about his comment, but God knew how we needed to learn.

There was a period of time that Bill and I were requested and consulted with whenever a person came to church that had a special need. We were the special needs ministry so we should be the ones that helped anyone with a disability, right? It became overwhelming for us when any child that had a behavior problem was sent our way. There were too many children to be able to accommodate and the volunteers were sending any uncomfortable situation our way. During that time, it occurred to us that this was one of the things Dad was talking about. We needed to affect the culture of the church in such a way that anyone serving in the church would be able to greet anyone with a challenge with compassion and grace. We couldn't have just two classrooms in the church that extended grace to the person with special needs, it needed to be the whole church. Once this happened, the ministry would start to disappear, because no matter where the person with a special need went in the church, they would be met with grace and acceptance.

Over time the church did grow and people with special needs were met with grace and support. In fact, if you look in the auditorium on a Sunday morning and watch the children's worship, you will have a hard time pointing out the children with special needs because they are such a part of the fabric of the church.

There were multitudes of leaders and Sunday school teachers that embraced the children with special needs. We all had a lot to learn, but there were enough key people on board to help change the DNA of the ministry. I wish I could name all of the staff and volunteers that embraced the ministry, but there are too many. To be honest, there were those that immediately understood because of their own personal experience, there were those that were hesitant, and there were those that dragged their feet, but God was moving the whole time!

Chapter Twenty-One

ERR ON GRACE

BILL AND I ARE NOW IN A NEW PHASE OF LIFE. We are in our 50s, we have shifted from being parents to being friends to our daughters, and we have welcomed grandchildren into our lives. At this stage in life, one of my favorite possessions is our kitchen table. It would probably be the first thing I would replace if we ever lost everything.

The table isn't fancy but it is nice and it is sturdy. By manipulating the leaves in the table it can be a variety of shapes. When we have an intimate group of four or want to play a card game, it can be made into a 4' x 4' square. When we have a group of six and want a little more class, it can be made into an oval. When we have a houseful and the family is together, it can be made into a wonderful circle where everyone is exchanging ideas, sharing laughter, and can be closely and lovingly engaged. I love my table!

The kitchen table has always been one of my favorite places. Over the years of my life, I have experienced teachable conversations, political debates, messy arguments and extensions of grace...all around the kitchen table. I dare to say it can be one of the most emotional and life-changing spots in the house.

Around the kitchen table, I have been blessed to be in the company of a variety of people and they have all touched my life in one way or another. Some of them have made me uncomfortable, some of them have even made me mad at times, but all of them have left an impression on me.

Both of my parents were very involved in politics and my mother even ran for County Commissioner when I was fourteen. I remember knocking on doors and walking in parades holding a banner for her. Politics were a part of my life from my earliest memories on.

Spiritually, I was raised in a Protestant denomination that some would consider liberal and others would consider conservative. It laid a spiritual foundation for my life and whenever I go back there, it is like going home. I love the ritual. I love the hymns. I love the memories.

As I grew older and moved on to college, my world broadened. I had been given the opportunity to experience a variety of people, but it had always been under the same framework of my parents and their beliefs. I started to question many things during those years. I needed to make my beliefs my own.

For the next twenty years, I remained involved in church but gradually became involved in more conservative denominations. I still loved people just as I always did. I had grown to love God with a depth I didn't know was possible. The conflict that grew in my heart, however, was discerning the lines between accountability and grace. I loved being spurred on in my spiritual growth and being held accountable for my commitment to God, but somewhere along the way, I felt like the grace was missing.

At one point, I contacted the pastor of my youth, Pastor Les Avery, through email and shared my struggle with him. He shared that he, too, had walked through this struggle. He said, "I have walked in legalism and I have walked in grace. Always err on grace." I so appreciated what he shared with me, but I still didn't understand it. It would take more experiences for me to be able to.

The last ten years of my life have been incredibly tough at times, but I now have a better understanding of what grace means. The concept of grace lives in my heart. I fully acknowledge that there are many dark corners left in my heart and I hope light will illuminate them soon, but nevertheless, grace lives in my heart.

One of the things that helped me the most with this is the decision to read some books written by people that think differently from me.

Doing this, however, required that I be at a place where I was not easily shaken or drawn away. But in reading the biographies of some people that think very differently from me politically, I have grown. Most often, I end up believing what I believe more strongly; however, I understand them better. I understand the difference in experiences that makes them think the way they do. I understand what makes them tick and I respect them. I guess when I read their book it is my way of having them at my kitchen table.

A month ago I had the privilege of having coffee with the pastor of my youth that I mentioned earlier. It was wonderful to hug him and see that familiar sparkle in his eyes.

I shared with him about the impact he had made on me as a child and the impact he had made on me through email eighteen years ago. He looked at me and smiled and said, "Always err on grace." Immediately what flashed in my mind was the way he closed every Sunday morning service:

"Be good to yourself and kind to your neighbor. Know that almost everyone you meet carries a heavy load. If you scratch beneath the surface of almost any life you will encounter pain. It is there. Don't be afraid to put your arm around your own shoulder or that of a friend. Go now in the love of Jesus and celebrate."

I smiled at Les, and as I did, he asked what I thought the most important thing in life was. Before I could answer he added, "Your answer is probably different from mine. Mine is not careers or anything like that. It is sitting around a cup of coffee like this and having dialogue."

Les Avery is now eighty-three years old. He recently took the gold in the 80-85-age category in the 2011 Senior Olympics for the 20k bike road race. He is a living example of grace, wisdom, commitment, and determination.

Having a cup of coffee with someone or inviting them to sit at your kitchen table breaks down the barriers. It takes away fear and takes away judgment. At a kitchen table, the wheelchair is less noticeable. At a kitchen table, a person's story is hopefully heard with grace.

I have to ask myself, when I am engaged in conversation with someone new at church (especially someone completely new to the church), am I making them feel like I am having a cup of coffee with them at my kitchen table, or am I making them feel like they are in front of a governing board being screened? Do I look at them and judge their appearance and abilities, or do I embrace them over a cup of coffee?

Chapter Twenty-Two

MOVING OUTWARD

THE LAST SEVERAL YEARS HAVE BEEN CHALLENGING FOR BILL and me. We were going through our own personal challenges and every day I felt more and more overwhelmed by the number of plates we were trying to keep spinning. For a while we managed to keep all of the plates spinning, but then they began to wobble and eventually a few of them fell. I felt increasingly overwhelmed and inadequate, convinced we were no longer doing what God wanted us to do.

We eventually shared with our leadership team how we were feeling and asked them to join us in prayer. We prayed that if we were to step away that God would bring someone forward to take over the ministry. I felt like a broken record whenever we had a leadership meeting as I asked for God's guidance. During those two years, we approached one of the people on our leadership team and asked her to pray about taking the lead. Each time, we asked, she said that she wasn't ready.

I often wondered if we should just step out and depend on God to fill in the gap. There were several people that thought we should set a date to transition out and trust God with the rest, but it never felt right. Our heart and soul was in this ministry. It felt like it would be stepping out of parenting before it was time. So we waited, and by faith and experience we knew that God would reveal His plan…eventually.

I have to be honest, during those two years, we just tried to maintain, and I asked God to forgive me for all of the things that I couldn't get done. There are so many nights that I would lie awake saddened by all of the wonderful things that should be happening but just weren't. The feelings of inadequacy were crippling at times. We just needed to hold on.

During that time, the requests for training steadily came in. We started off with inviting people to come to our trainings for new buddies and gradually the word got out and more churches started coming. Eventually, people that came to these trainings would call and ask if we would come to their church and train. Before we knew it we had forty-five churches that had attended our training. A church from College Station came, then a church from Dallas. Churches in Minnesota, New York and Indonesia requested materials. It became more and more obvious that God was moving us out of this ministry to move us forward and outward.

Please do not misunderstand me. This growth wasn't because of anything that Bill and I were doing. It was God moving in the church. We were simply trying to be obedient. It continues to blow my mind what God had in mind all along.

As the requests grew, we prayed even harder that God would reveal what should happen next. Do you remember the leader that we asked to take our place? She was suddenly laid off from the therapy center where she worked. She eventually felt led to take a part-time job to do in-house therapies. One evening we had our leadership meeting and none of the other leaders except for Terri could be there. We started the meeting with housekeeping announcements and then took prayer requests. I looked up at Terri and she said, "I am ready now." I don't know which emotion came first—shock or jubilation—but I was excited, and so was Bill. God had prepared the way for all of this to happen. We had a great meeting that night and were excited about the course God was laying out.

Terri had all of the skills and ideas that Bill and I were lacking to take the ministry to its next level. She has been an occupational therapist for fifteen years and had a huge heart for families and children affected by special needs. Terri's excitement has grown every week since then and so has ours. God has His timing and it is so worth the wait!! To top it off now God has provided a paid staff position for the ministry and a fabulous director has taken the reigns! God is good...so good.

I have to admit that Bill and I felt a huge sense of relief, mostly because we were so tired, but also because we knew that everything was on the right course again. We had no question in our minds that we were being called to move forward in training churches and encouraging the ones that had already gone through training. This was our next step.

Since handing off the ministry, it has been hard and we knew it would be. It felt like one of our children was leaving for college. We would no longer set the course. We would no longer be the ones to pick up the pieces should a mistake be made, and we would no longer decide the future. I will never forget the first two weeks after we announced the change. I felt invisible and out of place when we went to serve. No one asked me questions. It wasn't our baby anymore. To be honest, I went through a period of grieving, but I let myself. I knew it was okay to feel that way.

The next stage was when the entire children's ministry was told that we were stepping out and the panel of questions was directed to the new director of special needs ministry. It was hard, but it felt right.

Since then we have faced more challenges: the loss of Bill's brother, the loss of my brother, and a loved one's tragic car accident. We have only been able to hold a few trainings, but God seems to keep evolving the plan, or rather, disclosing the plans He had all along.

Several years ago God laid it on my heart to write this book. I wanted to share our journey with people so they could know the incredible blessing of serving in special needs ministry. I wanted them to be moved to serve this wonderful population of people and learn from the mistakes we had already made.

One day I was sharing with a close friend about my desire to write and she suggested I attend the Colorado Christian Writer's Conference in Estes Park, Colorado. I thought it was interesting, but thought no more about it. A few weeks later I was surfing the internet and looked up the website for the conference. They had a contest to win a partial scholarship based on what your writing project was about. I thought it would be interesting, so I entered the contest. Eventually I received an email letting me know that I had received a partial scholarship. I was excited about it and even more intrigued. I shared my crazy dream with my husband and left it at that.

A few weeks later, I was sharing about my love for writing with a friend, who is also the mother of one of my students. I told her about the conference. About a week later (I still can't believe this), the parents of all of my students handed me a card with $600 in it, and one of the parents gave me a plane ticket to Colorado. They wanted to support me in my dreams.

To say I was overwhelmed doesn't even express how I felt. God continually went before me during the entire conference. I met so many people that would help me grow and get direction for my dreams.

I am still not fully aware of what God's plans are, but I do know that I was to write this book. Only God knows what He wants to do from here.

CONCLUSION

THE LAST 16 YEARS HAVE BEEN AMAZING. They have been hard. They have been life changing and they have been wonderful. If I had to sum up the whole experience, though, I would have to say it has been humbling. How can you serve the God of the universe without being humbled? He is the creator of all things. He is the master of the heavens and the earth. He is God almighty. The very fact that He allows me to live and breathe is humbling enough, but He allows us to serve, to have purpose, and to bring glory to Him.

It is humbling that God chose Bill and me to be blessed. Our lives will never be the same because of the incredible children we have met along the way. Not only have we loved them unconditionally, but they have loved us unconditionally as well. They accepted our flaws, inadequacies and feeble attempts to teach them something, while the whole time they were teaching us.

The children that could not talk showed us that there are many ways to communicate. We didn't have the market on communication simply because we had voices. They showed us how to communicate with our eyes, our hands and even our posture.

The children that could not walk showed us there are many ways to approach the throne of grace. You don't have to necessarily use your eyes, voice, hand or even knees. We can approach the throne of grace simply with our hearts laid bare before Him.

The children that could not hear taught us to be more expressive. And the children that were not beautiful in the world's eyes ended up being the most beautiful in our eyes.

Our biggest advice about serving in special needs ministry is to come humbly to a group of people that will change your perspective more than you thought possible. Fall to your knees before God and say, "Teach me, Lord, for I know not what I do."

It is with great humility that we serve the Lord in a ministry that we are still learning and growing in. My hope is that, through sharing my heart with you, you have been moved. Maybe there will be a child that will come through the door of your church this week and you will look at them differently. Hopefully, you will not look at them with the fears of starting a new ministry, but with a heart of compassion that simply wants to embrace them and all that God has made them to be. I promise you the journey will be amazing and you will be both changed and blessed!

If you and or your church feel called to move into the area of special needs ministry and you would like to attend one of our trainings, please feel free to contact us at theboggi@aim.com or follow our blog, www.specialneeds-deana.blogspot.com. It is an exciting adventure to see what God is doing in the life and heart of His church. We would be blessed to share and grow together.

"You yourselves are our letter, written on our hearts, known and read by everybody. You show that you are a letter from Christ, the result of our ministry, written not with ink but with the Spirit of the living God, not on tablets of stone but on tablets of human hearts."
2 Corinthians 3:2 (NIV)

May God bless you in whatever area of ministry He calls you to.

Blessings,

Deana

ABOUT THE AUTHOR

Deana Boggess has served in Christian ministry for more than 30 years as a Sunday school teacher, administrator of women's ministry, preschool ministry coach, volunteer director, and director of special needs ministry. She is passionate about supporting and serving the family affected by special needs and inspiring and encouraging the local church to welcome, assimilate and nurture those affected by special needs into their church family. Deana currently serves as a bridge to kindergarten teacher and is blessed with a husband of 28 years, two daughters, two sons-in-law and two grandchildren.

15391885R00055

Made in the USA
Middletown, DE
04 November 2014